PENGUIN BOOKS

AMERICAN SHORT STORIES OF TODAY

AMERICAN
Short Stories of Today

Edited by Esmor Jones

PENGUIN BOOKS

PENGUIN BOOKS

Published by the Penguin Group
27 Wrights Lane, London W8 5TZ, England
Viking Penguin Inc., 40 West 23rd Street, New York, New York 10010, USA
Penguin Books Australia Ltd, Ringwood, Victoria, Australia
Penguin Books Canada Ltd, 2801 John Street, Markham, Ontario, Canada L3R 1B4
Penguin Books (NZ) Ltd, 182–190 Wairau Road, Auckland 10, New Zealand

Penguin Books Ltd, Registered Offices: Harmondsworth, Middlesex, England

First published 1988
10 9 8 7 6 5 4 3

Filmset in 10/11½ pt Linotron 202 Plantin

Typeset, printed and bound in Great Britain by
Hazell Watson & Viney Limited
Member of BPCC Limited
Aylesbury, Bucks, England

Contents

Introduction

There are fifteen short stories in this collection and, of course, they are all by American writers. To choose the stories for a book of this size is like picking a few apples from a tree groaning with fruit. However, you may get a taste for them!

Even so, the stories do come from quite a wide range of writers. Coast to coast, in fact, New York to Los Angeles! Though there are a couple of science fiction tales and one Western (both kinds of story much associated with America), I have found stories by young writers that tell us something about ordinary Americans and their lives. You will not find Dallas here but you will meet a lot of Americans coping with family life in farms, villages, towns and cities. There is sadness in some; there are smiles and laughter in others. I think you will see in all Americans, young and old, meeting life with toughness and, often, wisely. Authors and their characters come from all walks of life, too. A kid runs away from home; a farmer faces ruin; a baseball fanatic rescues the game he loves; a son watches his mother cope with hospital; an old man has a kind of love-hate relationship with his crusty old dog; a bore gets his come-uppance; children have rather too exciting a party; a small boy has to cope with knowing he accidentally shot and killed his older brother. It is about America, and America is different and immensely varied. But it is also about people, and they are much the same anywhere, aren't they?

ESMOR JONES

Star Light

Isaac Asimov is a scientist who became a writer of science fiction. His reputation is world-wide and his output enormous. He is particularly well-known for stories about robots. 'Star Light' seems to have a computer as a major 'character'. However, as Asimov never tires of telling us, it is human beings and not machines that cause tragedy and disaster. This truth, Trent, the escaping criminal, learns too late!

Arthur Trent heard them quite clearly. The tense, angry words shot out of his receiver.

'Trent! You can't get away. We will intersect your orbit in two hours and if you try to resist we will blow you out of space.'

Trent smiled and said nothing. He had no weapons and no need to fight. In far less than two hours the ship would make its jump through hyperspace and they would never find him. He would have with him nearly a kilogram of Krillium, enough for the construction of the brain-paths of thousands of robots and worth some ten million credits on any world in the Galaxy – and no questions asked.

Old Brennmeyer had planned the whole thing. He had planned it for thirty years and more. It had been his life's work.

'It's the getaway, young man,' he had said. 'That's why I need you. You can lift a ship off the ground and out into space. I can't.'

'Getting it into space is no good, Mr Brennmeyer,' Trent said. 'We'll be caught in half a day.'

'Not,' said Brennmeyer, craftily, 'if we make the Jump; not if we flash through and end up light-years away.'

hyperspace: space beyond. The 'Jump' will be the crossing over into another stellar system.

'It would take half a day to plot the Jump and even if we could take the time, the police would alert all stellar systems.'

'No, Trent, no.' The old man's hand fell on his, clutching it in trembling excitement. 'Not *all* stellar systems; only the dozen in our neighbourhood. The Galaxy is big and the colonists of the last fifty thousand years have lost touch with each other.'

He talked avidly, painting the picture. The Galaxy now was like the surface of man's original planet (Earth, they had called it) in prehistoric times. Man had been scattered over all the continents, but each group had known only the area immediately surrounding itself.

'If we make the Jump at random,' Brennmeyer said, 'we would be anywhere, even fifty thousand light-years away, and there would be no more chance of finding us than a pebble in a meteor swarm.'

Trent shook his head. 'And we don't find ourselves, either. We wouldn't have the foggiest way of getting to an inhabited planet.'

Brennmeyer's quick-moving eyes inspected the surroundings. No one was near him, but his voice sank to a whisper anyway. 'I've spent thirty years collecting data on every habitable planet in the Galaxy. I've searched all the old records. I've travelled thousands of light-years, farther than any space-pilot. And the location of every habitable planet is now in the memory store of the best computer in the world.'

Trent lifted his eyebrows politely.

Brennmeyer said, 'I design computers and I have the best. I've also plotted the exact location of every luminous star in the Galaxy, every star of spectral class of F, B, A, and O, and put that into the memory store. Once we've made the Jump the computer will scan the heavens spectroscopically and compare the results with the map of the Galaxy it contains. Once it finds the proper match, and sooner or later it will, the ship is located in space and it is then automatically guided through a second Jump to the neighbourhood of the nearest inhabited planet.'

'Sounds too complicated.'

'It can't miss. All these years I've worked on it and it can't miss. I'll have ten years left yet to be a millionaire. But you're young; you'll be a millionaire much longer.'

'When you Jump at random, you can end inside a star.'

'Not one chance in a hundred trillion, Trent. We might also land so far from any luminous star that the computer can't find anything to match up against its programme. We might find we've jumped only a light-year or two and the police are still on our trail. The chances of that are smaller still. If you want to worry, worry that you might die of a heart attack at the moment of take-off. The chances for that are much higher.'

'*You* might, Mr Brennmeyer. You're older.'

The old man shrugged. 'I don't count. The computer will do everything automatically.'

Trent nodded and remembered that. One midnight, when the ship was ready and Brennmeyer arrived with the Krillium in a briefcase (he had no difficulty, for he was a greatly trusted man) Trent took the briefcase with one hand while his other moved quickly and surely.

A knife was still the best, just as quick as a molecular depolariser, just as fatal, and much more quiet. Trent left the knife there with the body, complete with fingerprints. What was the difference? They wouldn't get him.

Deep in space now, with the police-cruisers in pursuit, he felt the gathering tension that always preceded a Jump. No physiologist could explain it, but every space-wise pilot knew what it felt like.

There was a momentary inside-out feeling as his ship and himself for one moment of non-space and non-time, became non-matter and non-energy, then reassembled itself instantaneously in another part of the Galaxy.

Trent smiled. He was still alive. No star was too close and there were thousands that were close enough. The sky was alive with stars and the pattern was so different that he knew the Jump had gone far. Some of those stars had to be spectral class F and better. The computer would have a nice, rich pattern to match against its memory. It shouldn't take long.

He leaned back in comfort and watched the bright pattern of starlight move as the ship rotated slowly. A bright star came into view, a really bright one. It didn't seem more than a couple of light-years away and his pilot's sense told him it was a hot one; good and hot. The computer would use that as its base and match the pattern centred about it. Once again, he thought: It shouldn't take long.

But it did. The minutes passed. Then an hour. And still the computer clicked busily and its lights flashed.

Trent frowned. Why didn't it find the pattern? The pattern had to be there. Brennmeyer had showed him his long years of work. He *couldn't* have left out a star or recorded it in the wrong place.

Surely stars were born and died and moved through space while in being, but these changes were slow, slow. In a million years, the patterns that Brennmeyer had recorded couldn't –

A sudden panic clutched at Trent. No! It *couldn't* be. The chances for it were even smaller than Jumping into a star's interior.

He waited for the bright star to come into view again, and, with trembling hands, brought it into telescopic focus. He put in all the magnification he could, and around the bright speck of light was the tell-tale fog of turbulent gases caught, as it were, in mid-flight.

It was a nova!

From dim obscurity, the star had raised itself to bright luminosity – perhaps only a month ago. It had graduated from a special class low enough to be ignored by the computer, to one that would be most certainly taken into account.

But the nova that existed in space didn't exist in the computer's memory store because Brennmeyer had not put it there. It had not existed when Brennmeyer was collecting his data – at least not as a luminous star.

'Don't count on it,' shrieked Trent. 'Ignore it.'

But he was shouting at automatic machinery that would match the nova-centred pattern against the Galactic pattern and find it nowhere and continue, nevertheless, to match and match and match for as long as its energy supply held out.

The air supply would run out much sooner. Trent's life would ebb away much sooner.

Helplessly, Trent slumped in his chair, watching the mocking pattern of star light and beginning the long and agonised wait for death.

– If he had only kept the knife.

---

nova: a new star. In fact, probably an old star suddenly bursting into brilliant life. Astronomers are familiar with this happening in the universe.

GINA BERRIAULT

The Stone Boy

Arnold and Eugie live with their parents on a farm in rural New York State,
not far from the small town of Corinth. The farm is just above the Hudson
River Valley in the foothills of the Adirondack Mountains, among lakes. This
is the setting for tragedy. The story is told from Arnold's point of view; he
is only nine. How can the grown-ups understand?

Was Arnold really a 'Stone Boy'?

Arnold drew his overalls and ravelling grey sweater over his naked
body. In the other narrow bed his brother Eugene went on sleeping,
undisturbed by the alarm clock's rusty ring. Arnold, watching his
brother sleeping, felt a peculiar dismay; he was nine, six years
younger than Eugie, and in their waking hours it was he who was
subordinate. To dispel emphatically his uneasy advantage over his
sleeping brother, he threw himself on the hump of Eugie's body.

'Get up! Get up!' he cried.

Arnold felt his brother twist away and saw the blankets lifted in
a great wing, and, all in an instant he was lying on his back under
the covers with only his face showing, like a baby, and Eugie was
sprawled on top of him.

'Whassa matter with you?' asked Eugie in sleepy anger, his face
hanging close.

'Get up,' Arnold repeated. 'You said you'd pick peas with me.'

Stupidly, Eugie gazed around the room as if to see if morning had
come into it yet. Arnold began to laugh derisively, making soft,
snorting noises, and was thrown off the bed. He got up from the
floor and went down the stairs, the laughter continuing, like hic-
cups, against his will. But when he opened the staircase door and

entered the parlour, he hunched up his shoulders and was quiet because his parents slept in the bedroom downstairs.

Arnold lifted his .22-caliber rifle from the rack on the kitchen wall. It was an old lever-action Winchester that his father had given him because nobody else used it any more. On their way down to the garden he and Eugie would go by the lake, and if there were any ducks on it he'd take a shot at them. Standing on the stool before the cupboard, he searched on the top shelf in the confusion of medicines and ointments for man and beast and found a small yellow box of .22 cartridges. Then he sat down on the stool and began to load his gun.

It was cold in the kitchen so early, but later in the day, when his mother canned the peas, the heat from the wood stove would be almost unbearable. Yesterday she had finished preserving the huckleberries that the family had picked along the mountain, and before that she had canned all the cherries his father had brought from the warehouse in Corinth. Sometimes, on these summer days, Arnold would deliberately come out from the shade where he was playing and make himself as uncomfortable as his mother was in the kitchen by standing in the sun until the sweat ran down his body.

Eugie came clomping down the stairs and into the kitchen, his head drooping with sleepiness. From his perch on the stool Arnold watched Eugie slip on his green knit cap. Eugie didn't really need a cap; he hadn't had a haircut in a long time and his brown curls grew thick and matted, close around his ears and down his neck, tapering there to a small whorl. Eugie passed his left hand through his hair before he set his cap down with his right. The very way he slipped his cap on was an announcement of his status; almost everything he did was a reminder that he was eldest – first he, then Nora, then Arnold – and called attention to how tall he was (almost as tall as his father), how long his legs were, how small he was in the hips, and what a neat dip above his buttocks his thick-soled logger's boots gave him. Arnold never tired of watching Eugie offer silent praise unto himself. He wondered, as he sat enthralled, if when he got to be Eugie's age he would still be undersized and his hair still straight.

Eugie eyed the gun. 'Don't you know this ain't duck-season?' he asked gruffly, as if he were the sheriff.

parlour: sitting room.

'No, I don't know,' Arnold said with a snigger.

Eugie picked up the tin washtub for the peas, unbolted the door with his free hand and kicked it open. Then, lifting the tub to his head, he went clomping down the back steps. Arnold followed, closing the door behind him.

The sky was faintly grey, almost white. The mountains behind the farm made the sun climb a long way to show itself. Several miles to the south, where the range opened up, hung an orange mist, but the valley in which the farm lay was still cold and colourless.

Eugie opened the gate to the yard and the boys passed between the barn and the row of chicken houses, their feet stirring up the carpet of brown feathers dropped by the moulting chickens. They paused before going down the slope to the lake. A fluky morning wind ran among the shocks of wheat that covered the slope. It sent a shimmer northward across the lake gently moving the rushes that formed an island in the centre. Killdeer, their white markings flashing, skimmed the water, crying their shrill, sweet cry. And there at the south end of the lake were four wild ducks, swimming out from the willows into open water.

Arnold followed Eugie down the slope, stealing, as his brother did, from one shock of wheat to another. Eugie paused before climbing through the wire fence that divided the wheatfield from the marshy pasture around the lake. They were screened from the ducks by the willows along the lake's edge.

'If you hit your duck, you want me to go in after it?' Eugie said.

'If you want,' Arnold said.

Eugie lowered his eyelids, leaving slits of mocking blue. 'You'd drown 'fore you got to it, them legs of yours are so puny,' he said.

He shoved the tub under the fence and, pressing down the centre wire, climbed through into the pasture.

Arnold pressed down the bottom wire, thrust a leg through and leaned forward to bring the other leg after. His rifle caught on the wire and he jerked at it. The air was rocked by the sound of the shot. Feeling foolish, he lifted his face, baring it to an expected shower of derision from his brother. But Eugie did not turn around. Instead, from his crouching position, he fell to his knees and then pitched forward onto his face. The ducks rose up crying from the

Killdeer: a large, North American species of Ring Plover.

lake, cleared the mountain background and beat away northward across the pale sky.

Arnold squatted beside his brother. Eugie seemed to be climbing the earth, as if the earth ran up and down, and when he found he couldn't scale it he lay still.

'Eugie?'

Then Arnold saw it, under the tendril of hair at the nape of the neck – a slow rising of bright blood. It had an obnoxious movement, like that of a parasite.

'Hey, Eugie,' he said again. He was feeling the same discomfort he had felt when he had watched Eugie sleeping; his brother didn't know that he was lying face down in the pasture.

Again he said, 'Hey, Eugie,' an anxious nudge in his voice. But Eugie was as still as the morning about them.

Arnold set his rifle on the ground and stood up. He picked up the tub and, dragging it behind him, walked along by the willows to the garden fence and climbed through. He went down on his knees among the tangled vines. The pods were cold with the night, but his hands were strange to him, and not until some time had passed did he realize that the pods were numbing his fingers. He picked from the top of the vine first, then lifted the vine to look underneath for pods and then moved on to the next.

It was a warmth on his back, like a large hand laid firmly there, that made him raise his head. Way up the slope the grey farmhouse was struck by the sun. While his head had been bent the land had grown bright around him.

When he got up his legs were so stiff that he had to go down on his knees again to ease the pain. Then, walking sideways, he dragged the tub, half full of peas, up the slope.

The kitchen was warm now; a fire was roaring in the stove with a closed-up, rushing sound. His mother was spooning eggs from a pot of boiling water and putting them into a bowl. Her short brown hair was uncombed and fell forward across her eyes as she bent her head. Nora was lifting a frying pan full of trout from the stove, holding the handle with a dish towel. His father had just come in from bringing the cows from the north pasture to the barn, and was sitting on the stool unbuttoning his red plaid Mackinaw.

'Did you boys fill the tub?' his mother asked.

'They ought of by now,' his father said. 'They went out of the house an hour ago. Eugie woke me up comin' down-stairs. I heard you shootin' – did you get a duck?'

'No,' Arnold said. They would want to know why Eugie wasn't coming in for breakfast, he thought. 'Eugie's dead,' he told them.

They stared at him. The pitch cracked in the stove.

'You kids playin' a joke?' his father asked.

'Where's Eugene?' his mother asked scoldingly. She wanted, Arnold knew, to see his eyes, and when he had glanced at her she put the bowl and spoon down on the stove and walked past him. His father stood up and went out the door after her. Nora followed them with little skipping steps, as if afraid to be left alone.

Arnold went into the barn, down along the foddering passage past the cows waiting to be milked, and climbed into the loft. After a few minutes he heard a terrifying sound coming toward the house. His parents and Nora were returning from the willows, and sounds sharp as knives were rising from his mother's breast and carrying over the sloping fields. In a short while he heard his father go down the back steps, slam the car door and drive away.

Arnold lay still as a fugitive, listening to the cows eating close by. If his parents never called him, he thought, he would stay up in the loft forever, out of the way. In the night he would sneak down for a drink of water from the faucet over the trough and for whatever food they left for him by the barn.

The rattle of his father's car as it turned down the lane recalled him to the present. He heard voices of his Uncle Andy and Aunt Alice as they and his father went past the barn to the lake. He could feel the morning growing heavier with sun. Someone, probably Nora, had let the chickens out of their coops and they were cackling in the yard.

After a while another car turned down the road off the highway. The car drew to a stop and he heard the voices of strange men. The men also went past the barn and down to the lake. The undertakers, whom his father must have phoned from Uncle Andy's house, had

---

ought of: spoken English; in talking more formally, it would be 'ought to have'. So, later in the story, we find *we'd of* ('we would have') and *I'd of* ('I would have').
faucet: tap.

arrived from Corinth. Then he heard everybody come back and heard the car turn around and leave.

'Arnold!' It was his father calling from the yard.

He climbed down the ladder and went out into the sun, picking wisps of hay from his overalls.

Corinth, nine miles away, was the county seat. Arnold sat in the front seat of the old Ford between his father, who was driving, and Uncle Andy; no one spoke. Uncle Andy was his mother's brother, and he had been fond of Eugie because Eugie had resembled him. Andy had taken Eugie hunting and had given him a knife and a lot of things, and now Andy, his eyes narrowed, sat tall and stiff beside Arnold.

Arnold's father parked the car before the courthouse. It was a two-storey brick building with a lamp on each side of the bottom step. They went up the wide stone steps, Arnold and his father going first, and entered the darkly panelled hallway. The shirt-sleeved man in the sheriff's office said that the sheriff was at Carlson's Parlour examining the Curwing boy.

Andy went off to get the sheriff while Arnold and his father waited on a bench in the corridor. Arnold felt his father watching him, and he lifted his eyes with painful casualness to the announcement, on the opposite wall, of the Corinth County Annual Rodeo, and then to the clock with its loudly clucking pendulum. After he had come down from the loft his father and Uncle Andy had stood in the yard with him and asked him to tell them everything, and he had explained to them how the gun had caught on the wire. But when they had asked him why he hadn't run back to the house to tell his parents, he had had no answer – all he could say was that he had gone down into the garden to pick the peas. His father had stared at him in a pale, puzzled way, and it was then that he had felt his father and the others set their cold, turbulent silence against him. Arnold shifted on the bench, his only feeling a small one of compunction imposed by his father's eyes.

county seat: the centre for local government.
sheriff: in the USA, the head of the local police force.
Carlson's Parlour: the room in an undertaker's or funeral director's premises where a body is laid out and looked after before the funeral. Mr Carlson is the undertaker.
Rodeo: A farmers' show where horse-riding and cattle-handling skills are the attraction.

At a quarter past nine Andy and the sheriff came in. They all went into the sheriff's private office, and Arnold was sent forward to sit in the chair by the sheriff's desk; his father and Andy sat down on the bench against the wall.

The sheriff lumped down into his swivel chair and swung toward Arnold. He was an old man with white hair like wheat stubble. His restless green eyes made him seem not to be in his office but to be hurrying and bobbing around somewhere else.

'What did you say your name was?' the sheriff asked.

'Arnold,' he replied; but he could not remember telling the sheriff his name before.

'Curwing?'

'Yes.'

'What were you doing with a .22, Arnold?'

'It's mine,' he said.

'Okay. What were you going to shoot?'

'Some ducks,' he replied.

'Out of season?'

He nodded.

'That's bad,' said the sheriff. 'Were you and your brother good friends?'

What did he mean – good friends? Eugie was his brother. That was different from a friend, Arnold thought. A best friend was your own age, but Eugie was almost a man. Eugie had a way of looking at him slyly and mockingly and yet confidentially, that had summed up how they both felt about being brothers. Arnold had wanted to be with Eugie more than with anybody else but he couldn't say they had been good friends.

'Did they ever quarrel?' the sheriff asked his father.

'Not that I know,' his father replied. 'It seemed to me that Arnold cared a lot for Eugie.'

'Did you?' the sheriff asked Arnold.

If it seemed so to his father, then it was so. Arnold nodded.

'Were you mad at him this morning?'

'No.'

'How did you happen to shoot him?'

'We was crawlin' through the fence.'

'Yes?'

'An' the gun got caught on the wire.'

'Seems the hammer must of caught,' his father put in.

'All right, that's what happened,' said the sheriff. 'But what I want you to tell me is this. Why didn't you go back to the house and tell your father right away? Why did you go and pick peas for an hour?'

Arnold gazed over his shoulder at his father, expecting his father to have an answer for this also. But his father's eyes, larger and even lighter blue than usual, were fixed upon him curiously. Arnold picked at a callus in his right palm. It seemed odd now that he had not run back to the house and wakened his father, but he could not remember why he had not. They were all waiting for him to answer.

'I came down to pick peas,' he said.

'Didn't you think,' asked the sheriff, stepping carefully from word to word, 'that it was more important for you to go tell your parents what had happened?'

'The sun was gonna come up,' Arnold said.

'What's that got to do with it?'

'It's better to pick peas while they're cool.'

The sheriff swung away from him, laid both hands flat on his desk. 'Well, all I can say is,' he said across to Arnold's father and Uncle Andy, 'he's either a moron or he's so reasonable that he's way ahead of us.' He gave a challenging snort. 'It's come to my notice that the most reasonable guys are mean ones. They don't feel nothing.'

For a moment the three men sat still. Then the sheriff lifted his hand like a man taking an oath. 'Take him home,' he said.

Andy uncrossed his legs. 'You don't want him?'

'Not now,' replied the sheriff. 'Maybe in a few years.'

Arnold's father stood up. He held his hat against his chest. 'The gun ain't his no more,' he said wanly.

Arnold went first through the hallway, hearing behind him the heels of his father and Uncle Andy striking the floor boards. He went down the steps ahead of them and climbed into the back seat of the car. Andy paused as he was getting into the front seat and gazed back at Arnold, and Arnold saw that his uncle's eyes had absorbed the knowingness from the sheriff's eyes. Andy and his father and the sheriff had discovered what made him go down into the garden. It was because he was cruel, the sheriff had said, and

gonna: going to.

didn't care about his brother. Was that the reason? Arnold lowered his eyelids meekly against his uncle's stare.

The rest of the day he did his tasks around the farm, keeping apart from the family. At evening, when he saw his father stomp tiredly into the house, Arnold did not put down his hammer and leave the chicken coop he was repairing. He was afraid that they did not want him to eat supper with them. But in a few minutes another fear that they would go to the trouble of calling him and that he would be made conspicuous by his tardiness made him follow his father into the house. As he went through the kitchen he saw the jars of peas standing in rows on the workbench, a reproach to him.

No one spoke at supper, and his mother, who sat next to him, leaned her head in her hand all through the meal, curving her fingers over her eyes so as not to see him. They were finishing their small, silent supper when the visitors began to arrive, knocking hard on the back door. The men were coming from their farms now that it was growing dark and they could not work any more.

Old Man Matthews, grey and stocky, came first, with his two sons, Orion, the elder, and Clint, who was Eugie's age. As the callers entered the parlour, where the family ate, Arnold sat down in a rocking chair. Even as he had been undecided before supper whether to remain outside or take his place at the table, he now thought that he should go upstairs, and yet he stayed to avoid being conspicuous by his absence. If he stayed, he thought, as he always stayed and listened when visitors came, they would see that he was only Arnold and not the person the sheriff thought he was. He sat with his arms crossed and his hands tucked into his armpits and did not lift his eyes.

The Matthews men had hardly settled down around the table, after Arnold's mother and Nora had cleared away the dishes, when another car rattled down the road and someone else rapped on the back door. This time it was Sullivan, a spare and sandy man, so nimble of gesture and expression that Arnold had never been able to catch more than a few of his meanings. Sullivan, in dusty jeans, sat down in the other rocker, shot out his skinny legs and began to talk in his fast way, recalling everything that Eugene had ever said to him. The other men interrupted to tell of occasions they remembered, and after a time Clint's young voice, hoarse like Eugene's had been, broke in to tell about the time Eugene had beat him in a wrestling match.

Out in the kitchen the voices of Orion's wife and of Mrs Sullivan mingled with Nora's voice but not, Arnold noticed, his mother's. Then dry little Mr Cram came, leaving large Mrs Cram in the kitchen, and there was no chair left for Mr Cram to sit in. No one asked Arnold to get up and he was unable to rise. He knew that the story had got around to them during the day about how he had gone and picked peas after he had shot his brother, and he knew that although they were talking only about Eugie they were thinking about him and if he got up, if he moved even his foot, they would all be alerted. Then Uncle Andy arrived and leaned his tall, lanky body against the doorjamb and there were two men standing.

Presently Arnold was aware that the talk had stopped. He knew without looking up that the men were watching him.

'Not a tear in his eye,' said Andy, and Arnold knew that it was his uncle who had gestured the men to attention.

'He don't give a hoot, is that how it goes?' asked Sullivan, trippingly.

'He's a reasonable fellow,' Andy explained. 'That's what the sheriff said. It's us who ain't reasonable. If we'd of shot our brother, we'd of come runnin' back to the house, cryin' like a baby. Well, we'd of been unreasonable. What would of been the use of actin' like that? If your brother is shot dead, he's shot dead. What's the use of gettin' emotional about it? The thing to do is go down to the garden and pick peas. Am I right?'

The men around the room shifted their heavy, satisfying weight of unreasonableness.

Matthews' son Orion said: 'If I'd of done what he done, Pa would've hung my pelt by the side of that big coyote's in the barn.'

Arnold sat in the rocker until the last man had filed out. While his family was out in the kitchen bidding the callers good-night and the cars were driving away down the dirt lane to the highway, he picked up one of the kerosene lamps and slipped quickly up the stairs. In his room he undressed by lamplight, although he and Eugie had always undressed in the dark, and not until he was lying in his bed did he blow out the flame. He felt nothing, not any grief.

Coyote: a prairie-wolf.

There was only the same immense silence and crawling inside of him; it was the way the house and fields felt under a merciless sun.

He awoke suddenly. He knew that his father was out in the yard, closing the doors of the chicken houses so that the chickens could not roam out too early and fall prey to the coyotes that came down from the mountains at daybreak. The sound that had wakened him was the step of his father as he got up from the rocker and went down the back steps. And he knew that his mother was awake in bed.

Throwing off the covers, he rose swiftly, went down the stairs and across the dark parlour to his parents' room. He rapped on the door.

'Mother?'

From the closed room her voice rose to him, a seeking and retreating voice. 'Yes?'

'Mother?' he asked insistently. He had expected her to realize that he wanted to go down on his knees by her bed and tell her that Eugie was dead. She did not know it yet, nobody knew it, and yet she was sitting up in bed, waiting to be told, waiting for him to confirm her dread. He had expected her to tell him to come in, to allow him to dig his head into her blankets and tell her about the terror he had felt when he had knelt beside Eugie. He had come to clasp her in his arms and, in his terror, to pommel her breasts with his head. He put his hand upon the knob.

'Go back to bed, Arnold,' she called sharply.

But he waited.

'Go back! Is night when you get afraid?'

At first he did not understand. Then, silently, he left the door and for a stricken moment stood by the rocker. Outside everything was still. The fences, the shocks of wheat seen through the window before him were so still it was as if they moved and breathed in the daytime and had fallen silent with the lateness of the hour. It was a silence that seemed to observe his father, a figure moving alone around the yard, his lantern casting a circle of light by his feet. In a few minutes his father would enter the dark house, the lantern still lighting his way.

Arnold was suddenly aware that he was naked. He had thrown off his blankets and come down the stairs to tell his mother how he felt about Eugie, but she had refused to listen to him and his nakedness had become unpardonable. At once he went back up the stairs, fleeing from his father's lantern.

At breakfast he kept his eyelids lowered as if to deny the humiliating night. Nora, sitting at his left, did not pass the pitcher of milk to him and he did not ask for it. He would never again, he vowed, ask them for anything, and he ate his fried eggs and potatoes only because everybody ate meals – the cattle ate, and the cats: it was customary for everybody to eat.

'Nora, you gonna keep that pitcher for yourself?' his father asked.

Nora lowered her head unsurely.

'Pass it on to Arnold,' his father said.

Nora put her hands in her lap.

His father picked up the metal pitcher and set it down at Arnold's plate.

Arnold, pretending to be deaf to the discord, did not glance up but relief rained over his shoulders at the thought that his parents recognized him again. They must have lain awake after his father had come in from the yard: had they realized together why he had come down stairs and knocked at their door?

'Bessie's missin' this morning,' his father called out to his mother, who had gone into the kitchen. 'She went up the mountain last night and had her calf, most likely. Somebody's got to go up and find her 'fore the coyotes get the calf.'

That had been Eugie's job, Arnold thought. Eugie would climb the cattle trails in search of a newborn calf and come down the mountain carrying the calf across his back, with the cow running down along behind him, mooing in alarm.

Arnold ate the few more forkfuls of his breakfast, put his hands on the edge of the table and pushed back his chair. If he went for the calf he'd be away from the farm all morning. He could switch the cow down the mountain slowly, and the calf would run along at its mother's side.

When he passed through the kitchen his mother was setting a kettle of water on the stove. 'Where you going?' she asked awkwardly.

'Up to get the calf,' he replied, averting his face.

'Arnold?'

At the door he paused reluctantly, his back to her, knowing that she was seeking him out, as his father was doing, and he called upon his pride to protect him from them.

'Was you knocking at my door last night?'

He looked over his shoulder at her, his eyes narrow and dry.

'What'd you want?' she asked humbly.

'I didn't want nothing,' he said flatly.

Then he went out the door and down the back steps, his legs trembling from the fright his answer gave him.

The Solipsist

Fredric Brown was perhaps best known in America for his mystery and science-fiction tales. But he also wrote oddly amusing and thought-provoking tales like this one. The second sentence of this brief fable is a pretty good dictionary definition of a 'solipsist'.

Walter B. Jehovah, for whose name I make no apology since it really *was* his name, had been a solipsist all his life. A solipsist, in case you don't happen to know the word, is one who believes that he himself is the only thing that really exists, that other people and the universe in general exist only in his imagination, and that if he quit imagining them they would cease to exist.

One day Walter B. Jehovah became a practising solipsist. Within a week his wife had run away with another man, he'd lost his job as a shipping clerk and he had broken his leg chasing a black cat to keep it from crossing his path.

He decided, in his bed at the hospital, to end it all.

Looking out the window, staring up at the stars, he wished them out of existence, and they weren't there any more. Then he wished all other people out of existence and the hospital became strangely quiet even for a hospital. Next, the world, and he found himself suspended in a void. He got rid of his body quite as easily and then took the final step of willing *himself* out of existence.

Nothing happened.

Strange, he thought, can there be a limit to solipsism?

'Yes,' a voice said.

'Who are you?' Walter B. Jehovah asked.

'I am the one who created the universe which you have just willed out of existence. And now that you have taken my place –' There was a deep sigh. '– I can finally cease my own existence, find oblivion, and let you take over.'

'But – how can *I* cease to exist? That's what I'm trying to do, you know.'

'Yes, I know,' said the voice. 'You must do it the same way *I* did. Create a universe. Wait until somebody in it really believes what you believed and wills it out of existence. Then you can retire and let him take over. Good-bye now.'

And the voice was gone.

Walter B. Jehovah was alone in the void and there was only one thing he could do. He created the heaven and the earth.

It took him seven days.

A Day in Town

Ernest Haycox (1899–1950) was a writer of Western stories. 'A Day in Town' is set in cattle country. But more and more people have been moving West. The new people are farmers not cattle ranchers. The homesteaders have a very hard time. As we see in this story of such a family, the problem is water and the solution is money – a loan from a bank. A loan is not easy to get and there is a family to care for.

They reached Two Dance around ten that morning and turned into the big lot between the courthouse and the Cattle King Hotel. Most of the homesteaders camped here when they came to town, for after a slow ride across the sage flats, underneath so hot and so yellow a sun, the shade of the huge locust trees was a comfort. Joe Blount unhitched and watered the horses and tied them to a pole. He was a long and loose and deliberate man who had worked with his hands too many years to waste motion, and if he dallied more than usual over his chores now it was because he dreaded the thing ahead of him.

His wife sat on the wagon's seat, holding the baby. She had a pin in her mouth and she was talking around it to young Tom: 'Stay away from the horses on the street and don't you go near the railroad tracks. Keep hold of May's hand. She's too little to be alone, you remember. Be sure to come back by noon.'

Young Tom was seven and getting pretty thin from growth. The trip to town had him excited. He kept nodding his sun-bleached head, he kept tugging at little May's hand, and then both of them

sage flats: near desert land where only the hardy sage brush grows readily.

ran headlong for the street and turned the corner of the Cattle King, shrilly whooping as they disappeared.

Blount looked up at his wife. She was a composed woman and not one to bother people with talk and sometimes it was hard for a man to know what was in her mind. But he knew what was there now, for all their problems were less than this one and they had gone over it pretty thoroughly the last two-three months. He moved his fingers up to the pocket of his shirt and dropped them immediately away, searching the smoky horizon with his glance. He didn't expect to see anything over there, but it was better than meeting her eyes at this moment. He said in his patiently low voice: 'Think we could make it less than three hundred?'

The baby moved its arms, its warm-wet fingers aimlessly brushing Hester Blount's cheeks. She said: 'I don't see how. We kept figuring – and it never gets smaller. You know best, Joe.'

'No,' he murmured, 'it never gets any smaller. Well, three hundred. That's what I'll ask for.' And yet, with the chore before him, he kept his place by the dropped wagon tongue. He put his hands in his pockets and drew a long breath and looked at the powdered earth below him with a sustained gravity, and was like this when Hester Blount spoke again. He noticed that she was pretty gentle with her words: 'Why, now, Joe, you go on. It isn't like you were shiftless and hadn't tried. He knows you're a hard worker and he knows your word's good. You just go ahead.'

'Guess we've both tried,' he agreed. 'And I guess he knows how it's been. We ain't alone.' He went out toward the street, reminding himself of this. They weren't alone. All the people along Christmas Creek were burned out, so it wasn't as if he had failed because he didn't know how to farm. The thought comforted him a good deal; it restored a little of his pride. Crossing the street toward Dunmire's stable, he met Chess Roberts, with whom he had once punched cattle on the Hat outfit, and he stopped in great relief and palavered with Chess for a good ten minutes until, looking back, he saw his wife still seated on the wagon. That sight vaguely troubled him and he drawled to Chess, 'Well, I'll see you later,' and turned quite slowly toward the bank.

There was nothing in the bank's old-fashioned room to take a

punched cattle: a cowboy's job – driving cattle.
palavered: chatted, talked.

man's attention. Yet when he came into its hot, shaded silence Joe Blount removed his hat and felt ill at ease as he walked toward Lane McKercher. There was a pine desk here and on the wall a railroad map showing the counties of the Territory in colours. Over at the other side of the room stood the cage where McKercher's son waited on the trade.

McKercher was big and bony and grey and his eyes could cut. They were that penetrating, as everybody agreed. 'Been a long time since you came to town. Sit down and have a talk,' and his glance saw more about Joe Blount than the homesteader himself could ever tell. 'How's Christmas Creek?'

Blount settled in the chair. He said, 'Why, just fine,' and laid his hands over the hat in his lap. Weather had darkened him and work had thinned him and gravity remained like a stain on his cheeks. He was, McKercher recalled, about thirty years old, had once worked as a puncher on Hat and had married a girl from a small ranch over in the Yellows. Thirty wasn't so old, yet the country was having its way with Joe Blount. When he dropped his head the skin around his neck formed a loose crease and his mouth had that half-severe expression which comes from too much trouble. This was what McKercher saw. This and the blue army shirt, washed and mended until it was as thin as cotton, and the man's long hard hands lying so loose before him.

McKercher said, 'A little dry over your way?'

'Oh,' said Blount, 'a little. Yeah, a little bit dry.'

The banker sat back and waited, and the silence ran on a long while. Blount moved around in the chair and lifted his hand and reversed the hat on his lap. His eyes touched McKercher and passed quickly on to the ceiling. He stirred again, not comfortable. One hand reached up to the pocket of his shirt, dropping quickly back.

'Something on your mind, Joe?'

'Why,' said Blount, 'Hester and I have figured it out pretty close. It would take about three hundred dollars until next crop. Don't see how it could be less. There'd be seed and salt for stock and grub to put in and I guess some clothes for the kids. Seems like a lot but we can't seem to figure it any smaller.'

'A loan?' said McKercher.

'Why, yes,' said Blount, relieved that the explaining was over.

'Now let's see. You've got another year to go before you get title to your place. So that's no security. How was your wheat?'

'Burned out. No rain over there in April.'

'How much stock?'

'Well, not much. Just two cows. I sold off last fall. The graze was pretty skinny.' He looked at McKercher and said in the briefest way, 'I got nothing to cover this loan. But I'm a pretty good worker.'

McKercher turned his eyes toward the desk. There wasn't much to be seen behind the cropped grey whiskers of his face. According to the country this was why he wore them – so that a man could never tell what he figured. But his shoulders rose and dropped and he spoke regretfully: 'There's no show for you on that ranch, Joe. Dry farming – it won't do. All you fellows are burned out. This country never was meant for it. It's cattle land and that's about all.'

He let it go like that, and waited for the homesteader to come back with a better argument. Only, there was no argument. Joe Blount's lips changed a little and his hands flattened on the peak of his hat. He said in a slow, mild voice. 'Well, I can see it your way all right,' and got up. His mind strayed up to the shirt pocket again, and fell away – and McKercher, looking straight into the man's eyes, saw an expression there hard to define. The banker shook his head. Direct refusal was on his tongue and it wasn't like him to postpone it, which he did. 'I'll think it over. Come back about two o'clock.'

'Sure,' said Blount, and turned across the room, his long frame swinging loosely, his knees springing as he walked, saving energy. After he had gone out of the place McKercher remembered the way the homesteader's hand had gone toward the shirt pocket. It was a gesture that remained in the banker's mind.

Blount stopped outside the bank. Hester, at this moment, was passing down toward the dry-goods store with the baby in her arms. He waited until she had gone into the store and then walked on toward the lower end of town, not wanting her to see him just then. He knew McKercher would turn him down at two o'clock. He had heard it pretty plainly in the banker's tone, and he was thinking of all the things he had meant to explain to McKercher. He was telling

dry-goods store: a general store selling clothes, hardware and some provisions.

McKercher that one or two bad years shouldn't count against a man. That the land on Christmas Creek would grow the best winter wheat in the world. That you had to take the dry with the wet. But he knew he'd never say any of this. The talk wasn't in him, and never had been. Young Tom and little May were across the street, standing in front of Swing's restaurant, seeing something that gripped their interest. Joe Blount looked at them from beneath the lowered brim of his hat; they were skinny with age and they needed some clothes. He went on by, coming against Chess Roberts near the saloon.

Chess said: 'Well, we'll have a drink on this.'

The smell of the saloon drifted out to Joe Blount, its odour of spilled whisky and tobacco smoke starting the saliva in his jaws, freshening a hunger. But Hester and the kids were on his mind and something told him it was unseemly, the way things were. He said: 'Not right now, Chess. I got some chores to tend. What you doing?'

'You ain't heard? I'm riding for Hat again.'

Blount said: 'Kind of quiet over my way. Any jobs for a man on Hat?'

'Not now,' said Chess. 'We been layin' off summer help. A little bit tough this year, Joe. You havin' trouble on Christmas Creek?'

'Me? Not a bit, Chess. We get along. It's just that I like to keep workin'.'

After Chess had gone, Joe Blount laid the point of his shoulder against the saloon wall and watched his two children walk hand in hand past the windows of the general store. Young Tom pointed and swung his sister around; and both of them had their faces against a window, staring in. Blount pulled his eyes away. It took the kids to do things that scraped a man's pride pretty hard, that made him feel his failure. Under the saloon's board awning lay shade, but sweat cracked through his forehead and he thought quickly of what he could do. Maybe Dunmire could use a man to break horses. Maybe he could get on hauling wood for the feed store. This was Saturday and the big ranch owners would be coming down the Two Dance grade pretty soon. Maybe there was a hole on one of those outfits. It was an hour until noon, and at noon he had to go back to Hester. He turned toward the feed store.

Hester Blount stood at the dry-goods counter of Vetten's store. Vetten came over, but she said, 'I'm just trying to think.' She laid the baby on the counter and watched it lift its feet straight in the air and aimlessly try to catch them with its hands; and she was thinking that the family needed a good many things. Underwear all around, and stockings and overalls. Little May had to have some material for a dress, and some ribbon. You couldn't let a girl grow up without a few pretty things, even out on Christmas Creek. It wasn't good for the girl. Copper-toed shoes for young Tom, and a pair for his father; and lighter buttoned ones for May. None of these would be less than two dollars and a half, and it was a crime the way it mounted up. And plenty of flannel for the baby.

She had not thought of herself until she saw the dark grey bolt of silk lying at the end of the counter, and when she saw it something happened to her heart. It wasn't good to be so poor that the sight of a piece of silk made you feel this way. She turned from it, ashamed of her thoughts – as though she had been guilty of extravagance. Maybe if she were young again and still pretty, and wanting to catch a man's eyes, it might not be so silly to think of clothes. But she was no longer young or pretty and she had her man. She could take out her love of nice things on little May, who was going to be a very attractive girl. As soon as Joe was sure of the three hundred dollars she'd come back here and get what they all had to have – and somehow squeeze out the few pennies for dress material and the hair ribbon.

She stood here thinking of these things and so many others – a tall and rather comely woman in her early thirties, darkfaced and carrying an even, sweet-lipped gravity while her eyes sought the dry-goods shelves and her hand unconsciously patted the baby's round middle.

A woman came bustling into the store and said in a loud, accented voice; 'Why, Hester Blount, of all the people I never expected to see!'

Hester said, 'Now, isn't this a surprise!' and the two took each other's hands, and fell into a quick half embrace. Ten years ago they had been girls together over in the Two Dance, Hester and this Lila Evenson who had married a town man. Lila was turning into a heavy woman and, like many heavy women, she loved white and wore it now, though it made her look big as a house. Above the tight collar of the dress, her skin was flushed red and a second chin faintly trembled when she talked. Hester Blount stood motionless, listening to that outpour of words, feeling the quick search of Lila's eyes.

Lila, she knew, would be taking everything in – her worn dress, her heavy shoes, and the lines of her face.

'And another baby!' said Lila and bent over it and made a long gurgling sound. 'What a lucky woman! That's three? But ain't it a problem, out there on Christmas Creek? Even in town here I worry so much over my one darling.'

'No,' said Hester, 'we don't worry. How is your husband?'

'So well,' said Lila. 'You know, he's bought the drugstore from old Kerrin, who is getting old. He had done so well. We are lucky, as we keep telling ourselves. And that reminds me. You must come up to dinner. You really must come this minute.'

They had been brought up on adjoining ranches and had ridden to the same school and to the same dances. But that was so long ago, and so much had changed them. And Lila was always a girl to throw her fortunes in other people's faces. Hester said, gently, regretfully: 'Now, isn't it too bad! We brought a big lunch in the wagon, thinking it would be easier. Joe has so many chores to do here.'

'I have often wondered about you, away out there,' said Lila. 'Have you been well? It's been such a hard year for everybody. So many homesteaders going broke.'

'We are well,' said Hester slowly, a small, hard pride in her tone. 'Everything's been fine.'

'Now, that's nice,' murmured Lila, her smile remaining fixed, but her eyes, Hester observed, were sharp and busy – and reading too much. Lila said, 'Next time you come and see us,' and bobbed her head and went out of the store, her clothes rustling in this quiet. Hester's lips went sharp-shut and quick colour burned on her cheeks. She took up the baby and turned into the street again and saw that Tom hadn't come yet to the wagon. The children were out of sight and there was nothing to do but wait. Hearing the far-off halloo of a train's whistle, she walked on under the board galleries to the depot.

Heat swirled around her and light flashed up from polished spots on the iron rails. Around her lay the full monotony of the desert, so familiar, so wide – and sometimes so hard to bear. Backed against the yellow depot wall, she watched the train rush forward, a high plume of white steam rising to the sky as it whistled to warn them. And then it rushed by, engine and cars, in a great smash of sound that stirred the baby in her arms. She saw men standing on the platforms. Women's faces showed in the car windows, serene and idly curious and not a part of Hester's world at all; and afterward the train was gone, leaving behind the heated smell of steel and smoke. When the quiet came back it was lonelier than before. She turned back to the wagon.

It was then almost twelve. The children came up, hot and weary and full of excitement. Young Tom said: 'The school is right in town. They don't have to walk at all. It's right next to the houses. Why don't they have to walk three miles like us?' And May said: 'I saw a china doll with real clothes and painted eyelashes. Can I have a china doll?'

Hester changed the baby on the wagon seat. She said: 'Walking is good for people, Tom. Why should you expect a doll now, May? Christmas is the time. Maybe Christmas we'll remember.'

'Well, I'm hungry.'

'Wait till your father comes,' said Hester.

When he turned in from the street, later, she knew something was wrong. He was always a deliberate man, not much given to smiling. But he walked with his shoulders down and when he came up he said only: 'I suppose we ought to eat.' He didn't look directly at her. He had his own strong pride and she knew this wasn't like him – to stand by the wagon's wheel, so oddly watching his children. She reached under the seat for the box of sandwiches and the cups and the jug of cold coffee. She said: 'What did he say, Joe?'

'Why, nothing yet. He said come back at two. He wanted to think about it.'

She murmured, 'It won't hurt us to wait,' and laid out the sandwiches. They sat on the shaded ground and ate, the children with a quick, starved impatience, with an excited and aimless talk. Joe Blount looked at them carefully. 'What was it you saw in the restaurant, sonny?'

'It smelled nice,' said young May. 'The smell came out the door.'

Joe Blount cleared his throat. 'Don't stop like that in front of the restaurant again.'

'Can we go now? Can we go down by the depot?'

'You hold May's hand,' said Blount, and watched them leave. He sat cross-legged before his wife, his big hands idle, his expression unstirred. The sandwich, which was salted bacon grease spread on

Hester's potato bread, lay before him. 'Ain't done enough this morning to be hungry,' he said.

'I know.'

They were never much at talking. And now there wasn't much to
say. She knew that he had been turned down. She knew that at two
o'clock he would go and come back empty-handed. Until then she
wouldn't speak of it, and neither would he. And she was thinking
with a woman's realism of what lay before them. They had nothing
except this team and wagon and two cows standing unfed in the
barn lot. Going back to Christmas Creek now would be going back
only to pack up and leave. For they had delayed asking for this loan
until the last sack of flour in the storehouse had been emptied.

He said: 'I been thinking. Not much to do on the ranch this fall.
I ought to get a little outside work.'

'Maybe you should.'

'Fact is, I've tried a few places. Kind of quiet. But I can look
around some more.'

She said, 'I'll wait here.'

He got up, a rangy, spare man who found it hard to be idle. He
looked at her carefully and his voice didn't reveal anything. 'If I
were you I don't believe I'd order anything at the stores until I come
back.'

She watched the way he looked out into the smoky horizon, the
way he held his shoulders. When he turned away, not meeting her
eyes, her lips made a sweet line across her dark face, a softly maternal
expression showing. She said, 'Joe,' and waited until he turned.
'Joe, we'll always get along.'

He went away again, around the corner of the Cattle King. She
shifted her position on the wagon's seat, her hand gently patting the
baby who was a little cross from the heat. One by one she went over
the list of necessary things in her mind, and one by one, erased
them. It was hard to think of little May without a ribbon bow in her
hair, without a good dress. Boys could wear old clothes, as long as
they were warm; but a girl, a pretty girl, needed the touch of nice-
ness. It was hard to be poor.

Coming out of the bank at noon, Lane McKercher looked into the corral space and saw the Blounts eating their lunch under the locust tree. He turned down Arapahoe Street, walking through the comforting shade of the poplars to the big square house at the end of the lane. At dinner hour his boy took care of the bank, and so he ate his meal with the housekeeper in a dining room whose shades had been tightly drawn – the heavy midday meal of a man who had developed his hunger and his physique from early days on the range. Afterward he walked to the living-room couch and lay down with a paper over his face for the customary nap.

A single fly made a racket in the deep quiet, but it was not this that kept him from sleeping. In some obscure manner the shape of Joe Blount came before him – the long, patient and work-stiffened shape of a man whose eyes had been so blue and so calm in face of refusal. Well, there had been something behind those eyes for a moment, and then it had passed away, eluding McKercher's sharp glance.

They were mostly all patient ones and seldom speaking – these men that came off the deep desert. A hard life had made them that way, as McKercher knew, who had shared that life himself. Blount was no different than the others and many times McKercher had refused these others, without afterthoughts. It was some other thing that kept his mind on Blount. Not knowing why, he lay quietly on the couch, trying to find the reason.

The country, he told himself, was cattle country, and those who tried to dry-farm it were bound to fail. He had seen them fail, year after year. They took their wagons and their families out toward Christmas Creek, loaded high with plunder; and presently they came back with their wagons baked and their eyebrows bleached and nothing left. With their wives sitting in the wagons, old from work, with their children long and thin from lack of food. They had always failed and always would. Blount was a good man, but so were most of the rest. Why should he be thinking of Blount?

He rose at one o'clock, feeling the heat and feeling his age; and washed his hands and face with good cold water. Lighting a cigar, he strolled back down Arapahoe and walked across the square toward the Cattle King. Mrs Blount sat on the wagon's seat, holding a baby. The older youngsters, he noticed, were in the cool runway of Dunmire's stable. He went into the saloon, though not to drink.

corral space: area where wagons and horses could be 'parked'.

'Nick,' he said, 'Joe Blount been in for a drink yet?'

The saloonkeeper looked up from an empty poker table, 'No,' he said.

McKercher went out, crossing to Billy Saxton's feed store. Deep in the big shed Billy Saxton weighed hay bales on his heavy scales. He stopped and sopped the sweat off his forehead, and smiled. 'Bankin', he stated, 'is easier.'

'Maybe it is,' said Lane McKercher. 'You know Joe Blount well?'

'Why, he's all right. Used to ride for Hat. Old man Dale liked him. He was in here a while back.'

'To buy feed?'

'No, he wanted to haul wood for me.'

McKercher went back up the street toward the bank. Jim Benbow was coming down the road from the Two Dance hills, kicking a long streamer of dust behind. Sun struck the windows on the north side of town, setting up a brilliant explosion of light. Joe Blount came out of the stable and turned over toward the Cattle King, waiting for Benbow.

In the bank, McKercher said to his son, 'All right, you go eat,' and sat down at his pine desk. Benbow put his head through the front door, calling: 'I'll need five thousand this week, Mac – until the stock cheque comes in.'

'All right.'

He sat quite still at the desk, stern with himself because he could not recall why he kept thinking of Joe Blount. Men were everything to Lane McKercher, who watched them pass along this street year in and year out, who studied them with his sharp eyes and made his judgements concerning them. If there was something in a man, it had to come out. And what was it in Joe Blount he couldn't name? The echoes of the big clock on the wall rattled around the droning silence of the bank like the echo of feet striking the floor; it was then a quarter of two, and he knew he had to refuse Blount a second time. He could not understand why he had not made the first turn-down final.

Blount met Jim Benbow on the corner of the Cattle King, directly after Hat's owner had left the bank. He shook Benbow's hand, warmed and pleased by the tall cattleman's smile of recognition. Benbow said: 'Been a long time since I saw you. How's Christmas Creek, Joe?'

'Fine – just fine. You're lookin' good. You don't get old.'

'Well, let's go have a little smile on that.'

'Why, thanks, no. I was wonderin'. It's pretty quiet on my place right now. Not much to do till spring. You need a man?'

Benbow shook his head. 'Not a thing doing, Joe. Sorry.'

'Of course – of course,' murmured Blount. 'I didn't figure there would be.'

He stood against the Cattle King's low porch rail after Benbow had gone down the street, his glance lifted and fixed on the smoky light of the desert beyond town. Shade lay around him but sweat began to creep below his hatbrim. He was closely and quickly thinking of places that might be open for a man, and knew there were none in town and none on the range. This was the slack season of the year. The children were over in front of the grocery store, stopped by its door, hand in hand, round, dark cheeks lifted and still. Blount swung his shoulders around, cutting them out of his sight.

Sullen Ben Drury came out of the courthouse and passed Blount, removing his cigar and speaking, and replacing the cigar again. Its smell was like acid biting at Blount's jaw corners, and suddenly he faced the bank with the odd and terrible despair of a man who has reached the end of hope, and a strange thought came to him, which was that the doors of that bank were wide open and money lay on the counter inside for the taking.

He stood very still, his head down, and after a while he thought: 'An unseemly thing for a man to hold in his head.' It was two o'clock then and he turned over the square, going toward the bank with his legs springing as he walked and all his muscles loose. In the quietness of the room his boots dragged up odd sound. He stood by Lane McKercher's desk, waiting without any show of expression; he knew what McKercher would say.

McKercher said, slowly and with an odd trace of irritation: 'Joe, you're wasting your time on Christmas Creek. And you'd waste the loan.'

Blount said, mildly and courteously: 'I can understand your view. Don't blame you for not loanin' without security.' He looked over McKercher's head, his glance going through the window to the far strip of horizon. 'Kind of difficult to give up a thing,' he mused. 'I figured to get away from ridin' for other folks and ride for myself.

Well, that was why we went to Christmas Creek. Maybe a place the kids could have later. Man wants his children to have somethin' better than he had.'

'Not on Christmas Creek,' said McKercher. He watched Joe Blount with a closer and sharper interest, bothered by a feeling he could not name. Bothered by it and turned impatient by it.

'Maybe, maybe not,' said Blount. 'Bad luck don't last forever.' Then he said, 'Well, I shouldn't be talkin'. I thank you for your time.' He put on his hat, and his big hand moved up across his shirt, to the pocket there – and dropped away. He turned toward the door.

'Hold on,' said Lane. 'Hold on a minute.' He waited till Blount came back to the desk. He opened the desk's drawer and pulled out a can of cigars, holding them up. 'Smoke?'

There was a long delay, and it was strange to see the way Joe Blount looked at the cigars, with his lips closely together. He said, his voice dragging on the words, 'I guess not, but thanks.'

Lane McKercher looked down at the desk, his expression breaking out of its maintained strictness. The things in a man had to come out, and he knew now why Joe Blount had stayed so long in his mind. It made him look up. 'I have been considering this. It won't ever be a matter of luck on Christmas Creek. It's a matter of water. When I passed the feed store today I noticed a second-hand windmill in the back. It will do. You get hold of Plummer Bodry and find out his price for driving you a well. I never stake a man unless I stake him right. We will figure the three hundred and whatever it takes to put up a tank and windmill. When you buy your supplies today, just say you've got credit here.'

'Why, now –' began Joe Blount in his slow, soft voice, 'I –'

But Lane McKercher said to his son, just coming back from lunch, 'I want you to bring your ledger over here.' He kept on talking and Joe Blount, feeling himself pushed out, turned and left the bank.

McKercher's son came over. 'Made that loan after all. Why?'

McKercher said only, 'He's a good man, Bob.' But he knew the real reason. A man that smoked always carried his tobacco in his shirt pocket. Blount had kept reaching, out of habit, for something that wasn't there. Well, a man like Blount loved this one small comfort and never went without it unless actually destitute. But Blount wouldn't admit it, and had been too proud to take a free cigar. Men were everything – and the qualities in them came out sooner or later, as with Blount. A windmill and water was a good risk with a fellow like that.

Hester watched him cross the square and come toward her, walking slowly, with his shoulders squared. She patted the baby's back and gently rocked it, and wondered at the change. When he came up he said, casually, 'I'll hitch and drive around to the store, so we can load the stuff you buy.'

She watched him carefully, so curious to know how it had happened. But she only said: 'We'll get along.'

He was smiling then, he who seldom smiled. 'I guess you need a few things for yourself. We can spare something for that.'

'Only a dress and some ribbon, for May. A girl needs something nice.' She paused, and afterward added, because she knew how real his need was, 'Joe, you buy yourself some tobacco.'

He let it out a long, long breath. 'I believe I will,' he said. They stood this way, both gently smiling. They needed no talk to explain anything to each other. They had been through so much these last few years. Hardship and trouble had drawn them so close together that words were unnecessary. So they were silent, remembering so much, and understanding so much, and still smiling. Presently he turned to hitch up.

SHIRLEY JACKSON

The Pajama Party

Shirley Jackson died in 1965; although young, she already had a remarkable reputation as a story writer. Some of her stories are haunting, even hair-raising. The pagan ritual of the very American village in 'The Lottery' convinced many Americans that the village in this modern morality tale actually existed. However, in 'The Pajama Party', there is a comic and down-to-earth family setting.

At a pajama party, the guests (all girls) stay the night.

It was planned by Jannie herself. I was won over reluctantly, by much teasing and promises of supernatural good behaviour; as a matter of fact Jannie even went so far as to say that if she could have a pajama party she would keep her room picked up for one solid month, a promise so far beyond the realms of possibility that I could only believe that she wanted the pajama party more than anything else in the world. My husband thought it was a mistake. 'You are making a terrible, an awful mistake,' he said to me. 'And don't try to say I didn't tell you so.' My older son Laurie told me it was a mistake. 'Man,' he said, '*this* you will regret. For the rest of your life you will be saying to yourself "Why did I let that dopey girl ever *ever* have a pajama party that night?" For the rest of your life. When you're an old lady you will be saying –'

'What can I do?' I said. 'I promised.' We were all at the breakfast table, and it was seven-thirty on the morning of Jannie's eleventh birthday. Jannie sat unhearing, her spoon poised blissfully over her cereal, her eyes dreamy with speculation over what was going to turn up in the packages to be presented that evening after dinner.

keep her room picked up: keep her room tidy.

Her list of wanted birthday presents had included a live pony, a pair of roller skates, high-heeled shoes of her very own, a make-up kit with real lipstick, a record player and records, and a dear little monkey to play with, and any or all of these things might be in the offing. She sighed, and set down her spoon, and sighed.

'You know of course,' Laurie said to me, 'I have the room right next to her? I'm going to be sleeping in there like I do every night? You know I'm going to be in my bed trying to sleep?' He shuddered. 'Giggle,' he said. 'Giggle, giggle, giggle, giggle, giggle, giggle. Two, three o'clock in the morning – giggle giggle giggle. A human being can't bear it.'

Jannie focused her eyes on him. 'Why don't we burn up this boy's birth certificate?' she asked.

'Giggle, giggle,' Laurie said.

Barry spoke, waving his toast. 'When Jannie gets her birthday presents can I play with it?' he asked. 'If I am very very careful can I please play with just the –'

Everyone began to talk at once to drown him out. 'Giggle, giggle,' Laurie shouted. 'Don't say I didn't warn you,' my husband said loudly. 'Anyway I promised,' I said. 'Happy birthday dear sister,' Sally sang. Jannie giggled.

'There,' Laurie said. 'You hear her? All night long – five of them.' Shaking his head as one who has been telling them and telling them and *telling* them not to bring that wooden horse through the gates of Troy, he stamped off to get his schoolbooks and his trumpet. Jannie sighed happily. Barry opened his mouth to speak and his father and Sally and I all said 'Shhh.'

Jannie had to be excused from her cereal, because she was too excited to eat. It was a cold frosty morning, and I forced the girls into their winter coats and warm hats, and put Barry into his snow suit. Laurie, who believes that he is impervious to cold, came downstairs, said, 'Mad, I tell you, mad,' sympathetically to me, ''By, cat,' to his father, and went out the back door toward his bike, ignoring my frantic insistence that he put on some kind of a jacket or at least a sweater.

I checked that teeth had been brushed, hair combed, handkerchiefs secured, told the girls to hold Barry's hand crossing the street, told Barry to hold the girls' hands crossing the street, put Barry's

mid-morning cookies into his jacket pocket, reminded Jannie for
the third time about her spelling book, held the dogs so they could
not get out when the door was opened, told everyone goodbye and
happy birthday again to Jannie, and watched from the kitchen window while they made their haphazard way down the driveway, lingering, chatting, stopping to point to things. I opened the door once
more to call to them to move along, they would be late for school,
and they disregarded me. I called to hurry *up*, and for a minute they
moved more quickly, hopping, and then came to the end of the
driveway and onto the sidewalk where they merged at once into the
general traffic going to school, the collection of red hoods and blue
jackets and plaid caps that goes past every morning and comes past
again at noontime and goes back after lunch and returns at last,
lingering, at three o'clock. I came back to the table and sat down
wearily, reaching for the coffeepot. 'Five of them are too many,' my
husband explained. 'One would have been quite enough.'

'You can't have a pajama party with just one guest,' I said sullenly.
'And anyway no matter who she invited the other three would have
been offended.'

By lunchtime I had set up four cots, two of them borrowed from
a neighbour who was flatly taken aback when she heard what I
wanted them for. 'I think you must be crazy,' she said. Jannie's
bedroom is actually two rooms, one small and one, which she calls
her library because her bookcase is in there, much larger. I put one
cot in her bedroom next to her bed, which left almost no room in
there to move around. The other three cots I lined up in her library,
making a kind of dormitory effect. Beyond Jannie's library is the
guest room, and all the bedrooms except Laurie's are on the other
side of the guest room. Laurie's room is separated by only the thin-
nest wall from Jannie's library. I used all my coloured sheets and
flowered pillowcases to make up the five beds, and every extra blanket in the house; I finally had to use the pillows from the couch.

When Jannie came home from school I made her lie down and
rest, pointing out in one of the most poignant understatements of
my life that she would probably be up late that night. In fifteen
minutes she was downstairs asking if she could get dressed for her
party. I said her party was not going to start until eight o'clock and

cookies: sweet biscuits.

to take an apple and go lie down again. In another ten minutes she was down to explain that she would probably be too excited to dress later and it would really be only common sense to put her party dress on now. I said if she came downstairs again before dinner was on the table I would personally call her four guests and cancel the pajama party. She finally rested for half an hour or so in the chair by the upstairs phone, talking to her friend Carole.

She was of course unable to eat her dinner, although she had chosen the menu. She nibbled at a piece of lamb, rearranged her mashed potatoes, and told her father and me that she could not understand how we had endured as many birthdays as we had. Her father said that he personally had gotten kind of used to them, and that as a matter of fact a certain quality of excitement did seem to go out of them after – say – thirty, and Jannie sighed unbelievingly.

'One more birthday like this would *kill* her,' Laurie said. He groaned. 'Carole,' he said, as one telling over a fearful list, 'Kate. Laura. Linda, Jannie. You must be *crazy*,' he said to me.

'I suppose your friends are so much?' Jannie said. 'I suppose Ernie didn't get sent down to Miss Corcoran's office six times today for throwing paper wads? I suppose Charlie –'

'You didn't seem to think Charlie was so bad, walking home from school,' Laurie said. 'I guess that wasn't *you* walking with –'

Jannie turned pink. 'Does my own brother have any right to insult me on my own birthday?' she asked her father.

In honour of Jannie's birthday Sally helped me clear the table, and Jannie sat in state with her hands folded, waiting. When the table was cleared we left Jannie there alone, and assembled in the study. While my husband lighted the candles on the pink-and-white cake, Sally and Barry took from the back of the closet the gifts they had chosen themselves and lovingly wrapped. Barry's gift was clearly a leathercraft set, since his most careful wrapping had been unable to make the paper go right round the box, and the name showed clearly. Sally had three books. Laurie had an album of records he had chosen himself ('This is for my *sister*,' he had told the clerk in the music store, most earnestly, with an Elvis Presley record in each hand, 'for my sister – not me, my *sister*'). Laurie also had to carry the little blue record player which my husband and I had decided was a more suitable gift for our elder daughter than a dear little monkey or even a pair of high-heeled shoes. I carried the boxes from the two sets of grandparents, one holding a flowered quilted skirt and a fancy blouse, and the other holding a stiff crinoline petticoat. With the cake leading, we filed into the dining room where Jannie sat. 'Happy birthday to you,' we sang, and Jannie looked once and then leaped past us to the phone. 'Be there in a minute,' she said, and then, 'Carole? Carole, listen, I *got* it, the record player. 'By.'

By a quarter to eight Jannie was dressed in the new blouse and skirt, over the petticoat. Barry was happily taking apart the leathercraft set, the record player had been plugged in and we had heard, more or less involuntarily, four sides of Elvis Presley. Laurie had shut himself in his room, dissociating himself utterly from the festivities. 'I was willing to *buy* them,' he explained, 'I even spent good money out of the bank, but no one can make me *listen*.'

I took a card table up to Jannie's room and squeezed it in among the beds; on it I put a pretty cloth and a bowl of apples, a small dish of candy, a plate of decorated cupcakes, and an ice bucket in which were five bottles of grape soda imbedded in ice. Jannie brought her record player upstairs and put it on the table and Laurie plugged it in for her on condition that she would not turn it on until he was safely back in his room. With what Laurie felt indignantly was an absolute and complete disregard for the peace of mind and healthy sleep of a cherished older son I put a deck of fortunetelling cards on the table, and a book on the meaning of dreams.

Everything was ready, and Jannie and her father and I were sitting apprehensively in the living room when the first guest came. It was Laura. She was dressed in a blue party dress, and she brought Jannie a charm bracelet which Jannie put on. Then Carole and Linda arrived together, one wearing a green party dress and the other a fancy blouse and skirt, like Jannie. They all admired Jannie's new blouse and skirt, and one of them had brought her a book and the other had brought a dress and hat for her doll. Kate came almost immediately afterward. She was wearing a wide skirt like Jannie's, and she had a crinoline, too. She and Jannie compared crinolines, and each of them insisted that the other's was much, *much* prettier. Kate had brought Jannie a pocketbook with a penny inside for luck. All the girls carried overnight bags but Kate, who had a small suit-

candy: sweets.

case. 'You'll think I'm going to stay for a *month*, the stuff I brought,' she said, and I felt my husband shudder.

Each of the girls complimented, individually, each item of apparel on each of the others. It was conceded that Jannie's skirt, which came from California, was of a much more advanced style than skirts obtainable in Vermont. The pocketbook was a most fortunate choice, they agreed, because it perfectly matched the little red flowers in Jannie's skirt. Laura's shoes were the prettiest anyone had *ever* seen. Linda's party dress was of orlon, which all of them simply *adored*. Linda said if she *did* say it herself, the ruffles never got limp. Carole was wearing a necklace which no one could *possibly* tell was not made of real pearls. Linda said that we had the *nicest* house, she was always telling her mother and father that she wished they had one just like it. My husband said we would sell any time. Kate said our dogs were just *darling*, and Laura said she *loved* that green chair. I said somewhat ungraciously that they had all of them spent a matter of thousands of hours in our house and the green chair was no newer or prettier than it had been the last time Laura was here, when she was bouncing up and down on the seat. Jannie said hastily that there were cupcakes and Elvis Presley records up in her room, and they were gone. They went up the back stairs like a troop of horses, saying 'Cupcakes, cupcakes'.

Sally and Barry were in bed, but permitted to stay awake because it was Friday night and Jannie's birthday. Barry had taken Jannie's leathercraft set up to his room, planning to make his dear sister a pair of moccasins. Because Sally and Barry were not invited to the party I took them each a tray with one cupcake, a glass of fruit juice, and three candies. Sally asked if she could play *her* phonograph while she read fairy tales and ate her cupcake and I said certainly, since in the general air of excitement prevailing I did not think that even Barry would fall asleep for a while yet. As I started downstairs Barry called after me to ask if *he* could play *his* phonograph and of course I could hardly say no.

When I got downstairs my husband had settled down to reading freshman themes in the living room. 'Everything seems . . .' he said; I believe he was going to finish 'quiet', but Elvis Presley started then from Jannie's room. There was a howl of fury from Laurie's

phonograph: record-player.

room, and then *his* phonograph started; to answer Elvis Presley he had chosen an old Louis Armstrong record, and he was holding his own. From the front of the house upstairs drifted down the opening announcement of 'Peter and the Wolf', from Sally, and then, distantly, from Barry's room the crashing chords which heralded (blast off!) 'Space Men on the Moon'.

'What did you say?' I asked my husband.

'Oh, when the saints, come marching in . . .'

'I said it seemed quiet,' my husband yelled.

'The cat, by a clarinet in a loooow register . . .'

'I want you, I need you . . .'

'Prepare for blast: five – four – three – two –'

'I want to be in their number . . .'

'It sure does,' I yelled back.

'Boom.' Barry's rocket was in space.

Barry took control for a minute, because he can sing every word of (blast off!) 'Space Men on the Moon', but then the wolf came pacing up to Peter's gate, Jannie switched to 'Blue Suede Shoes', and Laurie took out his trumpet. He played without a mute, ordinarily forbidden in the house, so for a few minutes he was definitely ascendant, even though a certain undeniable guitar beat intruded from Jannie, but then Jannie and her guests began to sing and Laurie faltered, lost the Saints, fell irresistibly into 'Blue Suede Shoes', cursed, picked up the Saints, and finally conceded defeat in time for four – three – two – one – Boom. Peter's gay strain came through clearly for a minute and then Jannie finished changing records and our house rocked to its foundations with 'Heartbreak Hotel'.

'Mommy,' Sally called down, 'I can't even hear the hunters coming.'

'Blast off!'

Laurie's door slammed and he came pounding down the back stairs and into the living room. He was carrying his record player and his trumpet. 'Dad,' he said pathetically.

His father nodded. 'Play the loudest,' he said.

'Got you, man.' They finally decided on Duke Ellington, and I went to sit in the kitchen with all the doors shut so that all I could hear was a kind of steady combined beat which shivered the window frames and got the pots and pans crashing together softly where they hung on the wall. When it got close to nine-thirty I came out to check on Sally and Barry, and found that Sally, fading but grim, had taken off 'Peter and the Wolf' and put on another record which featured a kind of laughing woodpecker, but she was getting sleepy. I told her good-night, and went on to Barry's room, where Barry had fallen asleep in his space suit somewhere on the dim craters of the moon, fragments of leather all over his bed. I closed his phonograph, covered him, and by the time I came back to Sally she was asleep, with her fairy-tale book open on her stomach and her kitten next to her cheek on the pillow. I put away her book, and moved the kitten to the foot of the bed, where he waited until I was convincingly on the stairs going down again and then moved softly, tiptoeing, back onto Sally's pillow. Sally wiggled comfortably, the kitten purred, and I went on downstairs to find Laurie and my husband relaxing over 'Take the A Train'.

Laurie was about to change the record when he hesitated, lifted his head, listened, and looked at his father. His father was listening too. The phonograph upstairs had stopped, and Laurie shook his head gloomily. 'Now it comes,' he said.

He was right.

After about half an hour I went to the foot of the back stairs and tried to call up to the girls to be quiet, but they could not hear me. They were apparently using the fortunetelling cards, because I could hear someone calling on a tall dark man and someone else remarking bitterly upon jealousy from a friend. I went halfway up the stairs and shouted, but they still could not hear me. I went to the top and pounded on the door and I could have been banging my head against a stone wall. I could hear the name of a young gentleman of Laurie's acquaintance being bandied about lightly by the ladies inside, coupled – I think – with Laura's name and references to a certain cake-sharing incident at recess, and insane shrieks, presumably from the maligned Laura. Then Kate brought up another name, joining it with Linda's, and the voices rose, Linda disclaiming. I banged both fists on the door, and there was silence for a second until someone said, 'Maybe it's your *brother*,' and there was a great screaming of 'Go away! Stay out! Don't come in!'

'Joanne,' I said, and there was absolute silence.

'Yes, mother?' said Jannie at last.

'May I come in?' I asked gently.

'Oh, yes,' said all the little girls.

I opened the door and went in. They were all sitting on the two beds in Jannie's room. The needle arm had been taken off the record, but I could see Elvis Presley going around and around. All the cupcakes were gone, and so was the candy. The fortunetelling cards were scattered over the two beds. Jannie was wearing her pink shortie pajamas, which were certainly too light for that cold night. Linda was wearing blue shortie pajamas. Kate was wearing college-girl-type ski pajamas. Laura was wearing a lace-trimmed nightgown, white, with pink roses. Carole was wearing yellow shortie pajamas. Their hair was mussed, their cheeks were pink, they were crammed uncomfortably together on to the two beds, and they were clearly awake long after their several bedtimes.

'Don't you think,' I said, 'that you had better get some sleep?'

'Oh, nooooo,' they all said, and Jannie added, 'The party's just *beginning*.' They were like a pretty bouquet of femininity, and I said – with what I knew Laurie would find a deplorable lack of firmness – that they could stay up for just a few minutes more.

'Dickie,' Kate whispered, clearly referring to some private joke, and all the little girls dissolved into helpless giggles, all except Carole, who cried out indignantly, 'I did *not*, I never *did*, I *don't*.'

Downstairs I said nostalgically to my husband and Laurie, 'I can remember, when I was about Jannie's age –'

'I just hope the neighbours are all asleep,' my husband said. 'Or maybe they just won't know it's coming from here.'

'Probably everyone in the neighbourhood saw those characters coming in,' Laurie said.

'Mommy,' Jannie said urgently from the darkness of the dining room. Startled, I hurried in.

'Listen,' she said, 'something's gone *terribly* wrong.'

'What's the matter?'

'Shh,' Jannie said. 'It's Kate and Linda. I thought they would both sleep in my library but now Kate isn't talking to Linda because Linda took her lunch box today in school and said she didn't and wouldn't give it back so now Kate won't sleep with Linda.'

'Well, then, why not put Linda –'

'Well, you see, I was going to have Carole in with me because really only don't tell the others, but really she's my *best* friend of all of them only now I can't put Kate and Linda together and –'

'Why not put one of them in with you?'

'Well, I *can't* put Carole in with Laura.'

'Why not?' I was getting tired of whispering.

'Well, because they *both* like Jimmy *Watson*.'

'Oh,' I said.

'And anyway Carole's wearing a shortie and Kate and Laura *aren't*.'

'Look,' I said, 'how about I sneak up right now through the front hall and make up the guest-room bed? Then you can put someone in there. Jimmy Watson, maybe.'

'*Mother*.' Jannie turned bright red.

'Sorry,' I said. 'Take a pillow from one of the beds in your library. Put someone in the guest room. Keep them busy for a few minutes and I'll have it ready. I just hope I have two more sheets.'

'Oh, *thank* you.' Jannie turned, and then stopped. 'Mother?' she said. 'Don't think from what I said that *I* like Jimmy Watson.'

'The thought never crossed my mind,' I said.

I raced upstairs and found two sheets; they were smallish, and not coloured, which meant that they were the very bottom of the pile, but as I closed the guest-room door behind me I thought optimistically that at least Jannie's problems were solved if I excepted Jimmy Watson and the dangerous rivalry of Carole, who is a natural platinum blonde.

Laurie played 'Muskrat Ramble'. Jannie came down to the dining room again in about fifteen minutes. 'Shh,' she said, when I came in to talk to her. 'Kate and Linda want to sleep together in the guest room.'

'But I thought you just said that Kate and Linda –'

'But they made up and Kate apologized for taking Linda's lunch box and Linda apologized for thinking she did, and they're all friends now except Laura is kind of mad because now Kate says she likes Harry Benson better.'

'Better than Laura?' I asked stupidly.

'Oh, *Mother*. Better than Jimmy Watson, of course. Except *I* think Harry Benson is goony.'

'If he was the one on patrol who let your brother Barry go across the street by himself he certainly *is* goony. As a matter of fact if there is one word I would automatically and instinctively apply to young Harry Benson it would surely be –'

'Oh, *Mother*. He is *not*.'

I had been kept up slightly past my own bedtime. 'All right,' I said. 'Harry Benson is not goony and it is fine with me if Kate and Carole sleep in the guest room if they don't –'

'Kate and *Linda*.'

'Kate and Linda. If they don't, if they *only* don't giggle any more.'

'*Thank* you. And may I sleep in the guest room too?'

'What?'

'It's a big bed. And we wanted to talk very quietly about –'

'Never mind,' I said. 'Sleep anywhere, but *sleep*.'

She was downstairs again about ten minutes later. Laurie and his father were eating crackers and cheese and discussing the probable derivation of 'cool', as in 'cool jazz'.

'Listen,' Jannie said in the dining room, 'can Kate sleep in the guest room too?'

'But I thought Kate was already –'

'Well, she was, but they couldn't sleep, because Kate *did* take Linda's lunch box and she broke the Thermos and Carole saw her so Carole told Linda and then Kate wouldn't let Carole in the guest room but I can't leave Carole with Laura because Laura said Carole's shortie pajamas were goony and Linda went and told her.'

'That was unkind of Linda,' I said, floundering.

'So then Carole said Linda –'

'Never mind,' I said. 'Just tell me who is sleeping where.'

'Well, Kate and I are sleeping in the guest room, because now everyone else is mad at Kate. And Carole is mad at Linda so Carole is sleeping in my room and Linda and Laura are sleeping in my library, except I just really don't know *what* will happen,' she sighed, 'if anyone tells Laura what Linda said about Jerry. Jerry Harper.'

'But can't Carole change with Linda and sleep with Laura?'

'Oh, *Mother*. You *know* about Carole and Laura and Jimmy Watson.'

'I guess I just forgot for a minute,' I said.

'Well,' Jannie said, 'I just thought I'd let you know where everyone was.'

About half-past one Laurie held up his hand and said, 'Listen.' I had been trying to identify the sensation, and thought it was like the sudden lull in a heavy wind which has been beating against the trees and the windows for hours, and then stops. 'Can it be possible?' my husband said.

Laurie began to put his records away, moving very softly. I went up the back stairs in my stocking feet, not making a sound, and opened the door to Jannie's room, easing it to avoid the slightest squeak.

Jannie was peacefully asleep in her own bed. The other bed in her room and the three beds in her library were empty. Reflecting upon the cataclysmic powers of Jimmy Watson's name, I found the four other girls all asleep on the guest-room bed. None of them was covered, but there was no way of putting a blanket over them without smothering somebody. I closed the window, and tiptoed away, and came downstairs to tell Laurie it was safe, he could go to bed now.

Then I got myself upstairs and fell into bed, and slept soundly until seventeen minutes past three by the bedroom clock, when I was awakened by Jannie.

'Kate feels sick,' she said. 'You've got to get up right away and take her home.'

W. P. KINSELLA

The Thrill of the Grass

W. P. Kinsella is a Canadian writer with a passion for baseball. He is certainly not alone in this, but there are few people who actually write baseball stories.

There was indeed a strike of professional baseball players in 1981 and all America felt deprived. As the narrator points out, what is there left to do except perhaps work longer?

The ballpark or stadium where the home team play has just been recovered with artificial grass, like many football grounds. This break with tradition is the heart of the story.

There are a number of baseball terms in the story:

shortstop: a fielder who stands by second base.

.217: the narrator hit 217 balls out of a hypothetical 1000 thrown during a season.

pitcher: the player who throws the ball to (or at!) the batsman. Pitching is a special skill.

bunt: to hit the ball lightly, rather than trying to hit it as far as possible: a surprise tactic.

catcher: the fielder standing behind the batter to catch the balls the batter fails to hit.

1981: the summer the baseball players went on strike. The dull weeks drag by, the summer deepens, the strike is nearly a month old. Outside the city the corn rustles and ripens in the sun. Summer without baseball: a disruption to the psyche. An unexplainable aimlessness engulfs me. I stay later and later each evening in the small office at the rear of my shop. Now, driving home after work, the worst of the rush-hour traffic over, it is the time of evening I would normally be heading for the stadium.

I enjoy arriving an hour early, parking in a far corner of the lot, walking slowly toward the stadium, rays of sun dropping softly over my shoulders like tangerine ropes, my shadow gliding with me, black as an umbrella. I like to watch young families beside their campers, the mothers in shorts, grilling hamburgers, their men drinking beer. I enjoy seeing little boys dressed in the home-team uniform, barely toddling, clutching hotdogs in upraised hands.

I am a failed shortstop. As a young man, I saw myself diving to my left, graceful as a toppling tree, fielding high grounders like a cat leaping for butterflies, bracing my right foot and tossing to first, the throw true as if a steel ribbon connected my hand and the first baseman's glove. I dreamed of leading the American League in hitting – being inducted into the Hall of Fame. I batted .217 in my senior year of high school and averaged 1.3 errors per nine innings.

I know the stadium will be deserted; nevertheless I wheel my car down off the freeway, park, and walk across the silent lot, my footsteps rasping and mournful. Strangle-grass and creeping charlie are already inching up through the gravel, surreptitious, surprised at their own ease. Faded bottle caps, rusted bits of chrome, an occasional paper clip, recede into the earth. I circle a ticket booth, sun-faded, empty, the door closed by an oversized padlock. I walk beside the tall, machinery-green, board fence. A half mile away a few cars hiss along the freeway; overhead a single-engine plane fizzes lazily. The whole place is silent as an empty classroom, like a house suddenly without children.

It is then that I spot the door-shape. I have to check twice to be sure it is there: a door cut in the deep green boards of the fence, more the promise of a door than the real thing, the kind of door, as children, we cut in the sides of cardboard boxes with our mother's paring knives. As I move closer, a golden circle of lock, like an acrimonious eye, establishes its certainty.

I stand, my nose so close to the door I can smell the faint odour of paint, the golden eye of a lock inches from my own eyes. My desire to be inside the ballpark is so great that for the first time in my life I commit a criminal act. I have been a locksmith for over

lot: car park.
freeway: motorway; there are several lanes each way and it is free because there are no toll charges.
strangle-grass and creeping charlie: weeds.

forty years. I take the small tools from the pocket of my jacket, and in less time than it would take a speedy runner to circle the bases I am inside the stadium. Though the ballpark is open-air, it smells of abandonment; the walkways and seating areas are cold as basements. I breathe the odours of rancid popcorn and wilted cardboard.

The maintenance staff were laid off when the strike began. Synthetic grass does not need to be cut or watered. I stare down at the ball diamond, where just to the right of the pitcher's mound, a single weed, perhaps two inches high, stands defiant in the rain-pocked dirt.

The field sits breathless in the orangy glow of the evening sun. I stare at the potato-coloured earth of the infield, that wide, dun arc, surrounded by plastic grass. As I contemplate the prickly turf, which scorches the thighs and buttocks of a sliding player as if he were being seared by hot steel, it stares back in its uniform ugliness. The seams that send routinely hit ground balls veering at tortuous angles are vivid, grey as scars.

I remember the ballfields of my childhood, the outfields full of soft hummocks and brown-eyed gopher holes.

I stride down from the stands and walk out to the middle of the field. I touch the stubble that is called grass, take off my shoes, but find it is like walking on a row of toothbrushes. It was an evil day when they stripped the sod from this ballpark, cut it into yard-wide swathes, rolled it, memories and all, into great green-and-black cinnamonroll shapes, trucked it away. Nature temporarily defeated. But Nature is patient.

Over the next few days an idea forms within me, ripening, swelling, pushing everything else into a corner. It is like knowing a new, wonderful joke and not being able to share. I need an accomplice.

I go to see a man I don't know personally, though I have seen his face peering at me from the financial pages of the local newspaper, and the *Wall Street Journal*, and I have been watching his profile at the baseball stadium, two boxes to the right of me, for several years. He is a fan. Really a fan. When the weather is intemperate, or the game not close, the people around us disappear like flowers closing at sunset, but we are always there until the last pitch. I know he is a man who attends because of the beauty and mystery of the game,

gopher: a North American burrowing rodent.
cinnamonroll: what in Britain is called a *Chelsea bun*, a type of Danish pastry.

a man who can sit during the last of the ninth with the game decided innings ago, and draw joy from watching the first baseman adjust the angle of his glove as the pitcher goes into his windup.

He, like me, is a first-base-side fan. I've always watched baseball from behind first base. The positions fans choose at sporting events are like politics, religion, or philosophy: a view of the world, a way of seeing the universe. They make no sense to anyone, have no basis in anything but stubbornness.

I brought up my daughters to watch baseball from the first-base side. One lives in Japan and sends me box scores from Japanese newspapers, and Japanese baseball magazines with pictures of superstars politely bowing to one another. She has a season ticket in Yokohama; on the first-base side.

'Tell him a baseball fan is here to see him,' is all I will say to his secretary. His office is in a skyscraper, from which he can look out over the city to where the prairie rolls green as mountain water to the limits of the eye. I wait all afternoon in the artificially cool, glassy reception area with its yellow and mauve chairs, chrome and glass coffee tables. Finally, in the late afternoon, my message is passed along.

'I've seen you at the baseball stadium,' I say, not introducing myself.

'Yes,' he says. 'I recognize you. Three rows back, about eight seats to my left. You have a red scorebook and you often bring your daughter . . .'

'Granddaughter. Yes, she goes to sleep in my lap in the late innings, but she knows how to calculate an ERA and she's only in Grade 2.'

'One of my greatest regrets,' says this tall man, whose moustache and carefully styled hair are polar-bear white, 'is that my grand-children all live over a thousand miles away. You're very lucky. Now, what can I do for you?'

'I have an idea,' I say. 'One that's been creeping toward me like a first baseman when the bunt sign is on. What do you think about artificial turf?'

'Hmmmf,' he snorts, 'that's what the strike should be about. Baseball is meant to be played on summer evenings and Sunday afternoons, on grass just cut by a horse-drawn mower,' and we smile as our eyes meet.

'I've discovered the ballpark is open, to me anyway,' I go on. 'There's no one there while the strike is on. The wind blows through the high top of the grandstand, whining until the pigeons in the rafters flutter. It's lonely as a ghost town.'

'And what is it you do there, alone with the pigeons?'

'I dream.'

'And where do I come in?'

'You've always struck me as a man who dreams. I think we have things in common. I think you might like to come with me. I could show you what I dream, paint you pictures, suggest what might happen . . .'

He studies me carefully for a moment, like a pitcher trying to decide if he can trust the sign his catcher has just given him.

'Tonight?' he says. 'Would tonight be too soon?'

'Park in the northwest corner of the lot about 1:00 a.m. There is a door about fifty yards to the right of the main gate. I'll open it when I hear you.'

He nods.

I turn and leave.

The night is clear and cotton warm when he arrives. 'Oh, my,' he says, staring at the stadium turned chrome-blue by a full moon. 'Oh, my,' he says again, breathing in the faint odours of baseball, the reminder of fans and players not long gone.

'Let's go down to the field,' I say. I am carrying a cardboard pizza box, holding it on the upturned palms of my hands, like an offering.

When we reach the field, he first stands on the mount, makes an awkward attempt at a windup, then does a little sprint from first to about half-way to second. 'I think I know what you've brought,' he says, gesturing toward the box, 'but let me see anyway.'

I open the box in which rests a square foot of sod, the grass smooth and pure, cool as a swatch of satin, fragile as baby's hair.

'Ohhh,' the man says, reaching out a finger to test the moistness of it. 'Oh, I see.'

We walk across the field, the harsh, prickly turf making the bottoms of my feet tingle, to the left-field corner where, in the angle formed by the foul line and the warning track, I lay down the square foot of sod. 'That's beautiful,' my friend says, kneeling beside me, placing his hand, fingers spread wide, on the verdant square, leaving a print faint as a veronica.

I take from my belt a sickle-shaped blade, the kind used for cutting carpet. I measure along the edge of the sod, dig the point in and pull carefully toward me. There is a ripping sound, like tearing an old bed sheet. I hold up the square of artificial turf like something freshly killed, while all the time digging the sharp point into the packed earth I have exposed. I replace the sod lovingly, covering the newly bared surface.

'A protest,' I say.

'But it could be more,' the man replies.

'I hoped you'd say that. It could be. If you'd like to come back . . .'

'Tomorrow night?'

'Tomorrow night would be fine. But there will be an admission charge . . .'

'A square of sod?'

'A square of sod two inches thick . . .'

'Of the same grass?'

'Of the same grass. But there's more.'

'I suspected as much.'

'You must have a friend . . .'

'Who would join us?'

'Yes.'

'I have two. Would that be all right?'

'I trust your judgement.'

'My father. He's over eighty,' my friend says. 'You might have seen him with me once or twice. He lives over fifty miles from here, but if I call him he'll come. And my friend . . .'

'If they pay their admission they'll be welcome . . .'

'And *they* may have friends . . .'

'Indeed they may. But what will we do with this?' I say, holding up the sticky-backed square of turf, which smells of glue and fabric.

'We could mail them anonymously to baseball executives, politicians, clergymen.'

veronica: a reference to the cloth St Veronica is said to have used to wipe Christ's face on the way to Calvary. There was left on the cloth a faint imprint. A veronica, then, is any such faint imprint.

'Gentle reminders not to tamper with Nature.'

We dance toward the exit, rampant with excitement.

'You will come back? You'll bring others?'

'Count on it,' says my friend.

They do come, those trusted friends, and friends of friends, each making a live, green deposit. At first, a tiny row of sod squares begins to inch along toward left-centre field. The next night even more people arrive, the following night more again, and the night after there is positively a crowd. Those who come once seem always to return accompanied by friends, occasionally a son or young brother, but mostly men my age or older, for we are the ones who remember the grass.

Night after night the pilgrimage continues. The first night I stand inside the deep green door, listening. I hear a vehicle stop; hear a car door close with a snug thud. I open the door when the sound of soft-soled shoes on gravel tells me it is time. The door swings silent as a snake. We nod curt greetings to each other. Two men pass me, each carrying a grasshopper-legged sprinkler. Later, each sprinkler will sizzle like frying onions as it wheels, a silver sparkler in the moonlight.

During the nights that follow, I stand sentinel-like at the top of the grandstand, watching as my cohorts arrive. Old men walking across a parking lot in a row, in the dark, carrying coiled hoses, looking like the many wheels of a locomotive, old men who have slipped away from their homes, skulked down their sturdy sidewalks, breathing the cool, grassy, after-midnight air. They have left behind their sleeping, grey-haired women, their immaculate bungalows, their manicured lawns. They continue to walk across the parking lot, while occasionally a soft wheeze, a nibbling, breathy sound like an old horse might make, divulges their humanity. They move methodically toward the baseball stadium which hulks against the moonblue sky like a small mountain. Beneath the tint of starlight, the tall light standards which rise above the fences and grandstand glow purple, necks bent forward, like sunflowers heavy with seed.

My other daughter lives in this city, is married to a fan, but one who watches baseball from behind third base. And like marrying outside the faith, she has been converted to the third-base side. They have their own season tickets, twelve rows up just to the outfield side of third base. I love her, but I don't trust her enough to let her in on my secret.

I could trust my granddaughter, but she is too young. At her age she shouldn't have to face such responsibility. I remember my own daughter, the one who lives in Japan, remember her at nine, all knees, elbows and missing teeth – remember peering in her room, seeing her asleep, a shower of well-thumbed baseball cards scattered over her chest and pillow.

I haven't been able to tell my wife – it is like my compatriots and I are involved in a ritual for true believers only. Maggie, who knew me when I still dreamed of playing professionally myself – Maggie, after over half a lifetime together, comes and sits in my lap in the comfortable easy chair which has adjusted through the years to my thickening shape, just as she has. I love to hold the lightness of her, her tongue exploring my mouth, gently as a baby's finger.

'Where do you go?' she asks sleepily when I crawl into bed at dawn.

I mumble a reply. I know she doesn't sleep well when I'm gone. I can feel her body rhythms change as I slip out of bed after midnight.

'Aren't you too old to be having a change of life,' she says, placing her toast-warm hand on my cold thigh.

I am not the only one with this problem.

'I'm developing a reputation,' whispers an affable man at the ballpark. 'I imagine any number of private investigators following any number of cars across the city. I imagine them creeping about the parking lot, shining pen-lights on licence plates, trying to guess what we're up to. Think of the reports they must prepare. I wonder if our wives are disappointed that we're not out discoing with frizzy-haired teenagers?'

Night after night, virtually no words are spoken. Each man seems to know his assignment. Not all bring sod. Some carry rakes, some hoes, some hoses, which, when joined together, snake across the infield and outfield, dispensing the blessing of water. Others, cradle in their arms bags of earth for building up the infield to meet the thick, living sod.

I often remain high in the stadium, looking down on the men moving over the earth, dark as ants, each sodding, cutting, watering, shaping. Occasionally the moon finds a knife blade as it trims the sod or slices away a chunk of artificial turf, and tosses the reflection skyward like a bright ball. My body tingles. There should be symphony music playing. Everyone should be humming 'America The Beautiful'.

Toward dawn, I watch the men walking away in groups, like small patrols of soldiers, carrying instead of arms, the tools and utensils which breathe life back into the arid ballfield.

Row by row, night by night, we lay the little squares of sod, moist as chocolate cake with green icing. Where did all the sod come from? I picture many men, in many parts of the city, surreptitiously cutting chunks out of their own lawns in the leafy midnight darkness, listening to the uncomprehending protests of their wives the next day – pretending to know nothing of it – pretending to have called the police to investigate.

When the strike is over I know we will all be here to watch the workouts, to hear the recalcitrant joints crackling like twigs after the forced inactivity. We will sit in our regular seats, scattered like popcorn throughout the stadium, and we'll nod as we pass on the way to the exits, exchange secret smiles, proud as new fathers.

For me, the best part of all will be the surprise. I feel like a magician who has gestured hypnotically and produced an elephant from thin air. I know I am not alone in my wonder. I know that rockets shoot off in half-a-hundred chests, the excitement of birthday mornings, Christmas eves, and home-town doubleheaders, boils within each of my conspirators. Our secret rites have been performed with love, like delivering a valentine to a sweetheart's door in that blue-steel span of morning just before dawn.

Players and management are meeting round the clock. A settlement is imminent. I have watched the stadium covered square foot by square foot until it looks like green graph paper. I have stood and felt the cool odours of the grass rise up and touch my face. I have studied the lines between each small square, watched those lines fade until they were visible to my eyes alone, then not even to them.

What will the players think, as they straggle into the stadium and find the miracle we have created? The old-timers will raise their heads like ponies, as far away as the parking lot, when the thrill of the grass reaches their nostrils. And, as they dress, they'll recall

doubleheaders: baseball games when there are two matches played one after the other.

sprawling in the lush outfields of childhood, the grass as cool as a mother's hand on a forehead.

'Good-bye, good-bye,' we say at the gate, the smell of water, of sod, of sweat, small perfumes in the air. Our secrets are safe with each other. We go our separate ways.

Alone in the stadium in the last chill darkness before dawn, I drop to my hands and knees in the centre of the outfield. My palms are sodden. Water touches the skin between my spread fingers. I lower my face to the silvered grass, which, wonder of wonders, already has the ephemeral odours of baseball about it.

URSULA LE GUIN

The Professor's Houses

Ursula Le Guin is another writer of science fiction and fantasy. But she is more than that. Her novels, though set in imaginary worlds, tell us of our own. She is also an author of books for children. *The Earthsea Trilogy* creates a world of magic and legend and also much more.

This story has an ordinary family setting in a university town. That is the outer world; we are taken into the inner world of the professor.

The professor had two houses, one inside the other. He lived with his wife and child in the outer house, which was comfortable, clean, disorderly, not quite big enough for all his books, her papers, their daughter's bright deciduous treasures. The roof leaked after heavy rains early in the fall before the wood swelled, but a bucket in the attic sufficed. No rain fell upon the inner house, where the professor lived without his wife and child, or so he said jokingly sometimes: 'Here's where I live. My house.' His daughter often added, without resentment, for the visitor's information, 'It started out to be for me, but it's really his.' And she might reach in to bring forth an inch-high table lamp with fluted shade, or a blue bowl the size of her little fingernail, marked 'Kitty' and half full of eternal milk; but she was sure to replace these, after they had been admired, pretty near exactly where they had been. The little house was very orderly, and just big enough for all it contained, though to some tastes the bric-a-brac in the parlour might seem excessive. The daughter's preference was for the store-bought gimmicks and appliances, the toasters and carpet sweepers of Lilliput, but she knew that most adult visitors would admire the perfection of the furnishings her father himself had so delicately and finely made and finished. He was inclined to be a little shy of showing off his own work, so she would point out the more ravishing elegances: the glass-fronted sideboard, the hardwood parquetry and the dadoes, the widow's walk. No visitor, child or adult, could withstand the fascination of the Venetian blinds, the infinitesimal slats that slanted and slid in perfect order on their cords of double-weight sewing thread. 'Do you know how to make a Venetian blind?' the professor would inquire, setting up the visitor for his daughter, who would forestall or answer the hesitant negative with a joyful 'Put his eyes out!' Her father, who was entertained by involutions and, like all teachers, willing to repeat a good thing, would then remark that after working for two weeks on those blinds he had established that a Venetian blind can also make an American blind.

'I did that awful rug in the nursery,' the professor's wife, Julia, might say, evidencing her participation in the inner house, her approbation, her incompetence. 'It's not up to Ian's standard, but he accepted the intent.' The crocheted rug was, in fact, coarse-looking and curly-edged; the needlepoint rugs in the other rooms, miniature Orientals and a gaudy floral in the master bedroom, lay flat and flawless.

The inner house stood on a low table in an open alcove, called 'The bookshelf end', of the long living room of the outer house. Friends of the family checked the progress of its construction, furnishing, and fitting out as they came to dinner or for a drink from time to time, from year to year. Occasional visitors assumed that it belonged to the daughter and was kept downstairs on display because it was a really fine doll's house, a regular work of art, and miniatures were coming into or recently had been in vogue. To certain rather difficult guests, including the dean of his college, the professor, without affirming or denying his part as architect, cabinetmaker, roofer, glazier, electrician, and *tapissier*, might quote Claude Lévi-Strauss. 'It's in *La Pensée Sauvage*, I think,' he would say. 'His idea is that the reduced model – the miniature – allows a knowledge of the whole to precede the knowledge of the parts. A

---

dadoes: border or pannelling over the lower half of the walls of a room.
widow's walk: a square, flat platform on top of a sloping roof surrounded by a railing. Traditionally, the wives of sailors would watch the ships coming in from here.
Claude Lévi-Strauss: French philosopher and critic. The argument is that we can see and understand a whole thing or idea from a model. We are not distracted by detail.

reversal of the usual process of knowing. Essentially, all the arts proceed that way, reducing a material dimension in favour of an intellectual dimension.' He found that persons entirely incapable of, and averse to, the kind of concrete thought that was his chief pleasure in working on the house went rigid as bird dogs at the name of the father of structuralism, and sometimes continued to gaze at the doll's house for some minutes with the tense and earnest gaze of a pointer at a sitting duck. The professor's wife had to entertain a good many strangers when she became state coordinator of the conservation organization for which she worked, but her guests, with urgent business on their minds, admired the doll's house perfunctorily if they noticed it at all.

As the daughter, Victoria, passed through the Vickie period and, at thirteen, entered upon the Tori period, her friends no longer had to be restrained or distracted from fiddling with the fittings of the little house, wearing out the fragile mechanisms, sometimes handling the furniture carelessly in their story games with its occupants. For there was, or had been, a family living in it. Victoria at eight had requested and received for Christmas a rather expensive European mama, papa, brother, sister, and baby, all cleverly articulated so that they could sit in the armchairs, and reach up to the copper-bottom saucepans hung above the stove, and hit or clasp one another in moments of passion. Family dramas of great intensity were enacted from time to time in the then incompletely furnished house. The brother's left leg came off at the hip and was never properly mended. Papa Bendsky received a marking-pen moustache and eyebrows that gave him an evil squint, like the half-breed lascar in an Edwardian thriller. The baby got lost. Victoria no longer played with the survivors; and the professor gratefully put them into the drawer of the table on which the house stood. He had always hated them, invaders, especially the papa, so thin, so flexible, with his nasty little Austrian-looking green jackets and his beady lascar eyes.

Victoria had recently bought with her earnings from baby-sitting a gift to the house and her father: a china cat to drink the eternal milk from the blue bowl marked 'Kitty'. The professor did not put the cat in the drawer. He believed it to be worthy of the house, as

Lascar: an Indian seaman.

the Bendsky family had never been. It was a finely modelled little figure, glazed tortoisehell on white. Curled on the hearth rug at twilight in the ruddy glow of the flames (red cellophane and a pen-light bulb), it looked very comfortable indeed. But since it lay curled up, it could never go into the kitchen to drink from the blue bowl; and this was evidently a trouble or burden to the professor's unconscious mind, for he had not exactly a dream about it, one night while he was going to sleep after working late on a complex and difficult piece of writing, a response he was to give to a paper to be presented later in the year at the A.A.A.S.; not a dream but a kind of half-waking experience. He was looking into or was in the kitchen of the inner house. That was not unusual, for when fitting the cabinets and wall panelling and building in the sink, he had become deeply familiar with the proportions and aspects of the kitchen from every angle, and had frequently and deliberately visualized it from the perspective of a six-inch person standing by the stove or at the pantry door. But in this case he had no sense of volition; he was merely there; and while standing there, near the big wood-burning stove, he saw the cat come in, look up at him, and settle itself down to drink the milk. The experience included the auditory: he heard the neat and amusing sound a cat makes lapping.

Next day he remembered this little vision clearly. His mind ran upon it, now and then. Walking across campus after a lecture, he thought with some intensity that it would be very pleasant to have an animal in the house, a live animal. Not a cat, of course, something very small. But his precise visual imagination at once presented him with a gerbil the size of the sofa, a monstrous hamster in the master bedroom, like the dreadful Mrs Bhoolabhoy in *Staying On*, billowing in the bed, immense, and he laughed inwardly, and winced away from the spectacle.

Once, indeed, when he had been installing the pull-chain toilet – the house and its furnishings were generally Victorian; that was the original eponymous joke – he had glanced up to see that a moth had got into the attic, but only after a moment of shock did he recognize it as a moth, the marvellous, soft-winged, unearthly owl beating there beneath the rafters. Flies, however, which often visited the house, brought only thoughts of horror movies and about professors

A.A.A.S.: American Academy of Applied Science.

who tampered with what man was not meant to know and ended up buzzing at the windowpane, crying vainly, 'Don't! No!' as the housewife's inexorable swatter fell. And serve them right. Would a ladybug do for a tortoise? The size was right, the colours wrong. The Victorians did not hesitate to paint live tortoises' shells. But tortoises do not raise their shell and fly away home. There was no pet suitable for the house.

Lately he had not been working much on the house; weeks and months went by before he got the tiny Landseer framed, and then it was a plain gilt frame fitted up on a Sunday afternoon, not the scrollwork masterpiece he had originally planned. Sketches for a glassed-in sun porch were never, as his dean would have put it, implemented. The personal and professional stresses in his department at the university, which had first driven him to this small escape hatch, were considerably eased under the new chairman; he and Julia had worked out their problems well enough to go on; and anyway the house and all its furnishings were done, in place, complete. Every armchair its antimacassars. Now that the Bendskys were gone, nothing got lost or broken, nothing even got moved. And no rain fell. The outer house was in real need of reroofing; it had required three attic buckets this October, and even so there had been some damage to the study ceiling. But the cedar shingles on the inner house were still blond, virginal. They knew little of sunlight, and nothing of the rain.

I could, the professor thought, pour water on the roof, to weather the shingles a bit. It ought to be sprinkled on, somehow, so it would be more like rain. He saw himself stand with Julia's green plastic half-gallon watering can at the low table in the book-lined alcove of the living room; he saw water falling on the little shingles, pooling on the table, dripping to the ancient but serviceable domestic Oriental rug. He saw a mad professor watering a toy house. Will it grow, Doctor? Will it grow?

That night he dreamed that the inner house, his house, was outside. It stood in a garden patch on a rickety support of some kind. The ground around it had been partly dug up as if for planting. The sky was low and dingy, though it was not raining yet. Some slats had come away from the back of the house, and he was worried

Landseer: a nineteenth-century painter of portraits and scenes from the Highlands of Scotland.

about the glue, 'I'm worried about the glue,' he said to the gardener or whoever it was that was there with a short-handled shovel, but the person did not understand. The house should not be outside, but it was outside, and it was too late to do anything about it.

He woke in great distress from this dream and could not find rest from it until his mind came upon the notion of, as it were, obeying the dream: actually moving the inner house outdoors, into the garden, which would then become the garden of both houses. An inner garden within the outer garden could be designed. Julia's advice would be needed for that. Miniature roses for hawthorn trees, surely. Scotch moss for the lawn? What could you use for hedges? She might know. A fountain? . . . He drifted back to sleep contentedly planning the garden of the house. And for months, even years, after that he amused or consoled himself from time to time, on troubled nights or in boring meetings, by reviving the plans for the miniature garden. But really it was not a practicable idea, given the rainy weather of his part of the world.

He and Julia got their house reroofed eventually, and brought the buckets down from the attic. The inner house was moved upstairs into Victoria's room when she went off to college. Looking into that room toward dusk of a November evening, the professor saw the peaked roofs and widow's walk sharp against the window light. They were still dry. Dust falls here, not rain, he thought. It isn't fair. He opened the front of the house and turned on the fireplace. The little cat lay curled up on the rug before the ruddy glow, the illusion of warmth, the illusion of shelter. And the dry milk in the half-full bowl marked 'Kitty' by the kitchen door. And the child gone.

BOBBIE ANN MASON

Graveyard Day

Bobbie Ann Mason lives in Pennsylvania and is now well-recognized as a novelist of distinction.

'Graveyard Day' is a kind of family story; the people are not all that well off – ordinary working Americans. Nothing much seems to happen except a rather unusual picnic at Joe's family graveyard. But what will the day and its small events lead to? Bobbie Ann Mason gets us to see and understand the doubts and confusion of Waldeen, whose life, like many people's, has had its problems.

Holly, swinging her legs from the kitchen stool, lectures her mother on natural foods. Holly is ten.

Waldeen says, 'I'll have to give your teacher a talking to. She's put notions in your head. You've got to have meat to grow.'

Waldeen is tenderizing liver, beating it with the edge of a saucer. Her daughter insists that she is a vegetarian. If Holly had said Rosicrucian, it would have sounded just as strange to Waldeen. Holly wants to eat peanuts, soyburgers, and yoghurt. Waldeen is sure this new fixation has something to do with Holly's father, Joe Murdock, although Holly rarely mentions him. After Waldeen and Joe were divorced last September, Joe moved to Arizona and got a construction job. Joe sends Holly letters occasionally, but Holly won't let Waldeen see them. At Christmas he sent Holly a copper Indian bracelet with unusual marks on it. It is Indian language, Holly tells her. Waldeen sees Holly polishing the bracelet while she is watching TV.

Waldeen shudders when she thinks of Joe Murdock. If he weren't

Rosicrucian: a small sect given to the occult.

Holly's father, she might be able to forget him. Waldeen was too young when she married him, and he had a reputation for being wild, which he did not outgrow. Now she could marry Joe McClain, who comes over for supper almost every night, always bringing something special, such as a roast or dessert. He seems to be oblivious to what things cost, and he frequently brings Holly presents. If Waldeen married Joe, then Holly would have a stepfather – something like a sugar substitute, Waldeen imagines. Shifting relationships confuse her. She doesn't know what marriage means anymore. She tells Joe they must wait. Her ex-husband is still on her mind, like the lingering after-effects of an illness.

Joe McClain is punctual, considerate. Tonight he brings fudge ripple ice cream and a half-gallon of Coke in a plastic jug. He kisses Waldeen and hugs Holly.

Waldeen says, 'We're having liver and onions, but Holly's mad 'cause I won't make Soybean Supreme.'

'Soybean *Delight*,' says Holly.

'Oh, excuse me!'

'Liver is full of poison. The poisons in the feed settle in the liver.'

'Do you want to stunt your growth?' Joe asks, patting Holly on the head. He winks at Waldeen and waves his walking stick at her playfully, like a conductor. Joe collects walking sticks and he has an antique one that belonged to Jefferson Davis. On a gold band, in italics, it says Jefferson Davis. Joe doesn't go anywhere without a walking stick, although he is only thirty. It embarrasses Waldeen to be seen with him.

'Sometimes a cow's liver just explodes from the poison,' says Holly. 'Poisons are *oozing* out.'

'Oh, Holly, hush, that's disgusting.' Waldeen plops the pieces of liver on to a plate of flour.

'There's this restaurant at the lake that has Liver Lovers' Night,' Joe says to Holly. 'Every Tuesday is Liver Lovers' Night.'

'Really?' Holly is wide-eyed, as if Joe is about to tell a long story, but Waldeen suspects Joe is bringing up the restaurant – Seas's Breeze at Kentucky Lake – to remind her that it was the scene of his proposal. Waldeen, not accustomed to eating out, studied the menu carefully, wavering between pork chops and T-bone steak

Jefferson Davis: President of the Confederate States during the American Civil War.

and then suddenly, without thinking, ordering catfish. She was disappointed to learn that the catfish was not even local, but frozen ocean cat. 'Why would they do that,' she kept saying, interrupting Joe, 'when they've got all the fresh channel cat in the world right here at Kentucky Lake?'

During supper, Waldeen snaps at Holly for sneaking liver to the cat, but with Joe gently persuading her, Holly manages to eat three bites of liver without gagging. Holly is trying to please him, as though he were some TV game show host who happened to live in the neighbourhood. In Waldeen's opinion, families shouldn't shift memberships, like clubs. But here they are, trying to be a family. Holly, Waldeen, Joe McClain. Sometimes Joe spends the weekend, but Holly prefers weekends at Joe's house because of his shiny wood floors and his parrot that tries to sing 'Inka Dinka Doo'. Holly likes the idea of packing an overnight bag.

Waldeen dishes out the ice cream. Suddenly inspired, she suggests a picnic Saturday. 'The weather's fairing up,' she says.

'I can't,' says Joe. 'Saturday's graveyard day.'

'Graveyard day?' Holly and Waldeen say together.

'It's my turn to clean off the graveyard. Every spring and fall somebody has to rake it off.' Joe explains that he is responsible for taking geraniums to his grandparents' graves. His grandmother always kept the pot in her basement during the winter, and in the spring she took it to her husband's grave, but she had died in November.

'Couldn't we have a picnic at the graveyard?' asks Waldeen.

'That's gruesome.'

'We never get to go on picnics,' says Holly. 'Or anywhere.' She gives Waldeen a look.

'Well, okay,' Joe says. 'But remember, it's serious. No fooling around.'

'We'll be real quiet,' says Holly.

'Far be it from me to disturb the dead,' Waldeen says, wondering why she is speaking in a mocking tone.

After supper, Joe plays rummy with Holly while Waldeen cracks pecans for a cake. Pecan shells fly across the floor, and the cat pounces on them. Holly and Joe are laughing together, whooping loudly over the cards. They sound like contestants on *Let's Make a Deal*. Joe Murdock wanted desperately to be on a game show and strike it rich. He wanted to go to California so he would have a chance to be on TV and so he could travel the freeways. He drove in the stock car races, and he had been drag racing since he learned to drive. Evel Knievel was his hero. Waldeen couldn't look when the TV showed Evel Knievel leaping over canyons. She told Joe many times, 'He's nothing but a showoff. But if you want to break your fool neck, then go right ahead. Nobody's stopping you.' She is better off without Joe Murdock. If he were still in town, he would do something to make her look foolish, such as paint her name on his car door. He once had WALDEEN painted in large red letters on the door of his LTD. It was like a tattoo. It is probably a good thing he is in Arizona. Still, she cannot really understand why he had to move so far away from home.

After Holly goes upstairs, carrying the cat, whose name is Mr Spock, Waldeen says to Joe, 'In China they have a law that the men have to help keep house.' She is washing dishes.

Joe grins. 'That's in China. This is *here*.'

Waldeen slaps at him with the dish towel, and Joe jumps up and grabs her. 'I'll do all the housework if you marry me,' he says. 'You can get the Chinese to arrest me if I don't.'

'You sound just like my ex-husband. Full of promises.'

'Guys named Joe are good at making promises.' Joe laughs and hugs her.

'All the important men in my life were named Joe,' says Waldeen, with pretended seriousness. 'My first real boyfriend was named Joe. I was fourteen.'

'You always bring that up,' says Joe. 'I wish you'd forget about them. You love *me* don't you?'

'Of course, you idiot.'

'Then why don't you marry me?'

'I just said I was going to think twice is all.'

'But if you love me, what are you waiting for?'

'That's the easy part. Love is easy.'

*

stock car races: the drivers use old cars and try to knock each other out of the way.
drag racing: races over only a quarter of a mile, where special cars test acceleration.
Evel Knievel: a well-known stunt driver.
LTD: a kind of car.

In the middle of *The Waltons*, C. W. Redmon and Betty Mathis drop by. Betty, Waldeen's best friend, lives with C.W., who works with Joe on a construction crew. Waldeen turns off the TV and clears magazines from the couch. C.W. and Betty have just returned from Florida and they are full of news about Sea World. Betty shows Waldeen her new tote bag with a killer whale pictured on it.

'Guess who we saw at the Louisville airport,' Betty says.

'I give up,' says Waldeen.

'Colonel Sanders!'

'He's eighty-four if he's a day,' C.W. adds.

'You couldn't miss him in that white suit,' Betty says. 'I'm sure it was him. Oh, Joe! He had a walking stick. He went strutting along –'

'No kidding!'

'He probably beats chickens to death with it,' says Holly, who is standing around.

'That would be something to have,' says Joe. 'Wow, one of the Colonel's walking sticks.'

'Do you know what I read in a magazine?' says Betty. 'That the Colonel Sanders outfit is trying to grow a three-legged chicken.'

'No, a four-legged chicken,' says C.W.

'Well, whatever.'

Waldeen is startled by the conversation. She is rattling ice cubes, looking for glasses. She finds an opened Coke in the refrigerator, but it may have lost its fizz. Before she can decide whether to open the new one Joe brought, C.W. and Betty grab glasses of ice from her and hold them out. Waldeen pours the Coke. There is a little fizz.

'We went first class the whole way,' says C.W. 'I always say, what's a vacation for if you don't splurge?'

'I thought we were going to buy *out* Florida,' says Betty. 'We spent a fortune. Plus, I gained a ton.'

'Man, those jumbo jets are really nice,' says C.W.

C.W. and Betty seem changed, exactly like all people who come back from Florida with tales of adventure and glowing tans, except

The Waltons: television series.
Colonel Sanders: the founder of the fast-food chain called *Kentucky Fried Chicken*. Advertisements for the company often show a drawing of a bearded distinguished-looking man in nineteenth-century dress.

that they did not get tans. It rained. Waldeen cannot imagine flying, or spending that much money. Her ex-husband tried to get her to go up in an airplane with him once – a $7.50 ride in a Cessna – but she refused. If Holly goes to Arizona to visit him, she will have to fly. Arizona is probably as far away as Florida.

When C.W. says he was going fishing on Saturday, Holly demands to go along. Waldeen reminds her about the picnic. 'You're full of wants,' she says.

'I just wanted to go somewhere.'

'I'll take you fishing one of these days soon,' says Joe.

'Joe's got to clean off his graveyard,' says Waldeen. Before she realizes what she is saying, she has invited C.W. and Betty to come along on the picnic. She turns to Joe, 'Is that okay?'

'I'll bring some beer,' says C.W. 'To hell with fishing.'

'I never heard of a picnic at a graveyard,' says Betty. 'But it sounds neat.'

Joe seems embarrassed. 'I'll put you to work,' he warns.

Later, in the kitchen, Waldeen pours more Coke for Betty. Holly is playing solitaire on the kitchen table. As Betty takes the Coke, she says, 'Let C.W. take Holly fishing if he wants a kid so bad.' She has told Waldeen that she wants to marry C.W., but she does not want to ruin her figure by getting pregnant. Betty pets the cat. 'Is that cat going to have kittens?'

Mr Spock, sitting with his legs tucked under his stomach, is shaped somewhat like a turtle.

'Heavens, no,' says Waldeen. 'He's just fat because I had him nurtured.'

'The word is *neutered!*' cries Holly, jumping up. She grabs Mr Spock and marches up the stairs.

'That youngun,' Waldeen says with a sigh. She feels suddenly afraid. Once, Holly's father, unemployed and drunk on whiskey and 7-Up, snatched Holly from the school playground and took her on a wild ride around town, buying her ice cream at the Tastee-Freez, and stopping at Newberry's to buy her an *All in the Family* Joey doll, with correct private parts. Holly was eight. When Joe brought her home, both were tearful and quiet. The excitement had worn off, but Waldeen had vividly imagined how it was. She wouldn't be surprised if Joe tried the same trick again, this time carrying Holly off to Arizona. She has heard of divorced parents who kidnap their own children.

The next day Joe McClain brings a pizza at noon. He is working nearby and has a chance to eat lunch with Waldeen. The pizza is large enough for four people. Waldeen is not hungry.

'I'm afraid we'll end up horsing around and won't get the grave-yard cleaned off,' Joe says. 'It's really a lot of work.'

'Why's it so important, anyway?'

'It's a family thing.'

'Family. Ha!'

'Why are you looking at me in that tone of voice?'

'I don't know what's what anymore,' Waldeen wails. 'I've got this kid that wants to live on peanuts and sleeps with a cat – and didn't even see her daddy at Christmas. And here *you* are, talking about family. What do you know about family? You don't know the half of it.'

'What's got into you lately?'

Waldeen tries to explain. 'Take Colonel Sanders, for instance. He was on *I've Got a Secret* once, years ago, when nobody knew who he was. His secret was that he had a million-dollar cheque in his pocket for selling Kentucky Fried Chicken to John Y. Brown. *Now* look what's happened. Colonel Sanders sold it but didn't get rid of it. He's still Colonel Sanders. John Y. sold it too and he can't get rid of it either. Everybody calls him the Chicken King, even though he's governor. That's not very dignified, if you ask me.'

'What in Sam Hill are you talking about? What's that got to do with families?'

'Oh, Colonel Sanders just came to mind because C.W. and Betty saw him. What I mean is, you can't just do something by itself. Everything else drags along. It's all *involved*. I can't get rid of my ex-husband just by signing a paper. Even if he *is* in Arizona and I never lay eyes on him again.'

Joe stands up, takes Waldeen by the hand, and leads her to the couch. They sit down and he holds her tightly for a moment. Waldeen has the strange impression that Joe is an old friend who moved away and returned, years later, radically changed. She doesn't understand the walking sticks, or why he would buy such an enormous pizza.

'One of these days you'll see,' says Joe, kissing her.

'See what?' Waldeen mumbles.

'One of these days you'll see. I'm not such a bad catch.'

Waldeen stares at a split in the wallpaper.

'Who would cut your hair if it wasn't for me?' he asks, rumpling her curls. 'I should have gone to beauty school.'

'I don't know.'

'Nobody else can do Jimmy Durante imitations like I can.'

'I wouldn't brag about it.'

On Saturday Waldeen is still in bed when Joe arrives. He appears in the doorway of her bedroom, brandishing a shiny black walking stick. It looks like a stiffened black racer snake.

'I overslept,' Waldeen says, rubbing her eyes. 'First I had insomnia. Then I had bad dreams. Then —'

'You said you'd make a picnic.'

'Just a minute. I'll go make it.'

'There's not time now. We've got to pick up C.W. and Betty.' Waldeen pulls on her jeans and a shirt, then runs a brush through her hair. In the mirror she sees blue pouches under her eyes. She catches sight of Joe in the mirror. He looks like an actor in a vaudeville show.

They go into the kitchen, where Holly is eating granola. 'She promised me she'd make carrot cake,' Holly tells Joe.

'I get blamed for everything,' says Waldeen. She is rushing around, not sure why. She is hardly awake.

'How could you forget?' asks Joe. 'It was your idea in the first place.'

'I didn't forget. I just overslept.' Waldeen opens the refrigerator. She is looking for something. She stares at a ham.

When Holly leaves the kitchen, Waldeen asks Joe, 'Are you mad at me?' Joe is thumping his stick on the floor.

'No, I just want to get this show on the road.'

'My ex-husband always said I was never dependable, and he was right. But *he* was one to talk. He had his head in the clouds.'

'Forget your ex-husband.'

Jimmy Durante: nicknamed 'Schnozzle' because of his large nose. He was a music-hall or burlesque comedian who appeared in a number of films in the 1930s.

'His name is Joe. Do you want some juice?' Waldeen is looking for orange juice, but she cannot find it.

'No.' Joe leans on his stick. 'He's over and done with. Why don't you just cross him off your list?'

'Why do you think I had bad dreams? Answer me that. I must be afraid of *something*.'

There is no juice. Waldeen closes the refrigerator door. Joe is smiling at her enigmatically. What she is really afraid of, she realizes, is that he will turn out to be just like Joe Murdock. But it must be only the names, she reminds herself. She hates the thought of a string of husbands, and the idea of a stepfather is like a substitute host on a talk show. It makes her think of Johnny Carson's many substitute hosts.

'You're just afraid to do anything new, Waldeen,' Joe says. 'You're afraid to cross the street. Why don't you get your ears pierced? Why don't you adopt a refugee? Why don't you get a dog?'

'You're crazy. You say the weirdest things.' Waldeen searches the refrigerator again. She pours a glass of Coke and watches it foam.

It is afternoon before they reach the graveyard. They had to wait for C.W. to finish painting his garage door, and Betty was in the shower. On the way, they bought a bucket of fried chicken. Joe said little on the drive into the country. When he gets quiet, Waldeen can never figure out if he is angry or calm. When he put the beer cooler in the trunk, she caught a glimpse of the geraniums in an ornate concrete pot with a handle. It looked like a petrified Easter basket. On the drive, she closed her eyes and imagined that they were in a funeral procession.

The graveyard is next to the woods on a small rise fenced in with barbed wire. A herd of Holsteins grazes in the pasture nearby, and in the distance the smokestacks of the new industrial park send up lazy swirls of smoke. Waldeen spreads out a blanket, and Betty opens beers and hands them around. Holly sits down under a tree, her back to the gravestones, and opens a Vicki Barr flight stewardess book.

Joe won't sit down to eat until he has unloaded the geraniums.

Johnny Carson: a well-known presenter of a talk or chat-show on American television.
Holsteins: a breed of cattle, here referring to the herd of cows.

He fusses over the heavy basket, trying to find a level spot. The flowers are not yet blooming.

'Wouldn't plastic flowers keep better?' asks Waldeen. 'Then you wouldn't have to lug that thing back and forth.' There are several bunches of plastic flowers on the graves. Most of them have fallen out of their containers.

'Plastic, yuck!' cries Holly.

'I should have known I'd say the wrong thing,' says Waldeen.

'My grandmother liked geraniums,' Joe says.

At the picnic, Holly eats only slaw and the crust from a drumstick. Waldeen remarks, 'Mr Spock is going to have a feast.'

'You've got a treasure, Waldeen,' says C.W. 'Most kids just want to load up on junk.'

'Wonder how long a person can survive without meat?' says Waldeen, somewhat breezily. Suddenly, she feels miserable about the way she treats Holly. Everything Waldeen does is so round-about, so devious, a habit she is sure she acquired from Joe Murdock. Disgusted, Waldeen flings a chicken bone out among the graves. Once, her ex-husband wouldn't bury the dog that was hit by a car. It lay in a ditch for over a week. She remembers Joe saying several times, 'Wonder if the dog is still there?' He wouldn't admit that he didn't want to bury it. Waldeen wouldn't do it because he had said he would do it. It was a war of nerves. She finally called the Highway Department to pick it up. Joe McClain, at least, would never be that barbaric.

Joe pats Holly on the head and says, 'My girl's stubborn, but she knows what she likes.' He makes a Jimmy Durante face that causes Holly to smile. Then he brings out a surprise for her, a bag of trail mix, which includes pecans and raisins. When Holly pounces on it, Waldeen notices that Holly is not wearing the Indian bracelet her father gave her. Waldeen wonders if there are vegetarians in Arizona.

Blue sky burns through the intricate spring leaves of the maples on the fence line. The light glances off the gravestones – a few thin slabs that date back to the last century and eleven sturdy blocks of marble and granite. Joe's grandmother's grave is a brown heap.

Waldeen opens another beer. She and Betty are stretched out under a maple tree and Holly is reading. Betty is talking idly about the diet she intends to go on. Waldeen feels too lazy to move. She watches the men work. While C.W rakes leaves, Joe washes off the gravestones with water he brought in a camp carrier. He scrubs out the carvings with a brush. He seems as devoted as a man washing and polishing his car on a Saturday afternoon. Betty plays he-loves-me-he-loves-me-not with the fingers of a maple leaf. The fragments fly away in a soft breeze.

From her Sea World tote bag, Betty pulls out playing cards with Holly Hobbie pictures on them. The old-fashioned child with the bonnet hiding her face is just the opposite of Waldeen's own strange daughter. Waldeen sees Holly secretly watching the men. They pick up their beer cans from a pink, shiny tombstone and drink a toast to Joe's great-great-grandfather Joseph McClain, who was killed in the Civil War. His stone, almost hidden in dead grasses, says 1841–1862.

'When I die, they can burn me and dump the ashes in the lake,' says C.W.

'Not me,' says Joe. 'I want to be buried right here.'

'*Want* to be? You planning to die soon?'

Joe laughs. 'No, but if it's my time, then it's my time. I wouldn't be afraid to go.'

'I guess that's the right way to look at it.'

Betty says to Waldeen, 'He'd marry me if I'd have his kid.'

'What made you decide you don't want a kid, anyhow?' Waldeen is shuffling the cards, fifty-two identical children in bonnets.

'Who says I decided? You just do whatever comes natural. Whatever's right for you.' Betty has already had three beers and she looks sleepy.

'Most people do just the opposite. They have kids without thinking. Or get married.'

'Talk about decisions,' Betty goes on. 'Did you see *60 Minutes* when they were telling about Palm Springs? And how all those rich people live? One woman had hundreds of dresses and Morley Safer was asking her how she ever decided what on earth to wear. He was *strolling* through her closet. He could have played *golf* in her closet.'

'Rich people don't know beans,' says Waldeen. She drinks some beer, then deals out the cards for a game of hearts. Betty snatches each card eagerly. Waldeen does not look at her own cards right away. In the pasture, the cows are beginning to move. The sky is losing its blue. Holly seems lost in her book, and the men are laughing. C.W. stumbles over a footstone hidden in the grass and falls on to a grave. He rolls over, curled up with laughter.

'Y'all are going to kill yourselves,' Waldeen says, calling to him across the graveyard.

Joe tells C.W. to shape up. 'We've got work to do,' he says.

Joe looks over at Waldeen and mouths something. 'I love you'? Her ex-husband used to stand in front of the TV and pantomime singers. She suddenly remembers a Ku Klux Klansman she saw on TV. He was being arrested at a demonstration, and as he was led away in handcuffs, he spoke to someone off-camera, ending with a solemn message, 'I *love* you.' He was acting for the camera, as if to say, 'Look what a nice guy I am.' He gave Waldeen the creeps. That could have been Joe Murdock, Waldeen thinks. Not Joe McClain. Maybe she is beginning to get them straight in her mind. They have different ways of trying to get through to her. The differences are very subtle. Soon she will figure them out.

Waldeen and Betty play several hands of hearts and drink more beer. Betty is clumsy with the cards and loses three hands in a row. Waldeen cannot keep her mind on the cards either. She wins accidentally. She can't concentrate because of the graves, and Joe standing there saying 'I love you.' If she marries Joe, and doesn't get divorced again, they will be buried here together. She picks out a likely spot and imagines the headstone and the green carpet and the brown leaves that will someday cover the twin mounds. Joe and C.W. are bringing leaves to the centre of the graveyard and piling them on the place she has chosen. Waldeen feels peculiar, as if the burial plot, not a diamond ring, symbolizes the promise of marriage. But there is something comforting about the thought, which she tries to explain to Betty.

'Ooh, that's gross,' says Betty. She slaps down a heart and takes the trick.

Waldeen shuffles the cards for a long time. The pile of leaves is growing dramatically. Joe and C.W. have each claimed a side of the graveyard, and they are racing. It occurs to Waldeen that she has spent half her life watching guys named Joe show off for her. Once, when Waldeen was fourteen, she went out on to the lake with Joe

Ku Klux Klan: a racist organization infamous for its attacks on black people.

Suiter in a rented pedal boat. When Waldeen sees him at the bank, where he works, she always remembers the pedal boat and how they stayed out in the silver-blue lake all afternoon, ignoring the people waving them in from the shore. When they finally returned, Joe owed ten dollars in overtime on the boat, so he worked Saturdays, mowing yards, to pay for their spree. Only recently in the bank, when they laughed over the memory, he told her that it was worth it, for it was one of the great adventures of his life, going out in a pedal boat with Waldeen, with nothing but the lake and time.

Betty is saying, 'We could have a nice bonfire and a wienie roast – what *are* you doing?'

Waldeen has pulled her shoes off. And she is taking a long, running start, like a pole vaulter, and then with a flying leap she lands in the immense pile of leaves, up to her elbows. Leaves are flying and everyone is standing around her, forming a stern circle, and Holly, with her book closed on her fist, is saying, 'Don't you know *any*thing?'

Victrola

Well, the dog was called Victrola – after a label on a gramophone record! ('How could a person give a dog such a name?') Bundy wondered. People sometimes wondered which of the two would go first. In the meantime, though, old man and old dog went their separate ways together.

'Sit!' said Bundy, although the dog already sat. His knowing what Bundy would say was one of the things people noticed about their close relationship. The dog sat – not erect, like most dogs, but off to one side, so that the short-haired pelt on one rump was always soiled. When Bundy attempted to clean it, as he once did, the spot no longer matched the rest of the dog, like a cleaned spot on an old rug. A second soiled spot was on his head, where children and strangers liked to pat him. Over his eyes the pelt was so thin his hide showed through. A third defacement had been caused by the leash in his younger years, when he had tugged at it harder, sometimes almost gagging as Bundy resisted.

Those days had been a strain on both of them. Bundy developed a bad bursitis, and the crease of the leash could still be seen on the back of his hand. In the past year, over the last eight months, beginning with the cold spell in December, the dog was so slow to cross the street Bundy might have to drag him. That brought on spells of angina for Bundy, and they would both have to stand there until they felt better. At such moments the dog's slantwise gaze was one that Bundy avoided. 'Sit!' he would say, no longer troubling to see if the dog did.

bursitis: an inflamed swelling.

The dog leashed to a parking meter, Bundy walked through the drugstore to the prescription counter at the rear. The pharmacist, Mr Avery, peered down from a platform two steps above floor level – the source of a customer's still-pending lawsuit. His gaze to the front of the store, he said, 'He still itching?'

Bundy nodded. Mr Avery had recommended a vitamin supplement that some dogs found helpful. The scratching had been replaced by licking.

'You've got to remember,' said Avery, 'he's in his nineties. When you're in your nineties, you'll also do a little scratchin'!' Avery gave Bundy a challenging stare. If Avery reached his nineties, Bundy was certain Mrs Avery would have to keep him on a leash or he would forget who he was. He had repeated this story about the dog's being ninety ever since Bundy had first met him and the dog was younger.

'I need your expertise,' Bundy said. (Avery lapped up that sort of flattery.) 'How does five cc.'s compare with five hundred mg.'s?'

'It doesn't. Five cc.'s is a liquid measure. It's a spoonful.'

'What I want to know is, how much vitamin C am I getting in five cc.'s?'

'Might not be any. In a liquid solution, vitamin C deteriorates rapidly. You should get it in the tablet.' It seemed clear he had expected more of Bundy.

'I see,' said Bundy. 'Could I have my prescription?'

Mr Avery lowered his glasses to look for it on the counter. Bundy might have remarked that a man of Avery's age – and experience – ought to know enough to wear glasses he could both see and read through, but having to deal with him once a month dictated more discretion than valour.

Squinting to read the label, Avery said, 'I see he's upped your dosage.' On their first meeting, Bundy and Avery had had a sensible discussion about the wisdom of minimal medication, an attitude that Bundy thought was unusual to hear from a pharmacist.

'His point is,' said Bundy, 'since I like to be active, there's no reason I shouldn't enjoy it. He tells me the dosage is still pretty normal.'

'Hmm,' Avery said. He opened the door so Bundy could step behind the counter and up to the platform with his Blue Cross card. For the umpteenth time he told Bundy, 'Pay the lady at the front. Watch your step as you leave.'

As he walked toward the front Bundy reflected that he would rather be a little less active than forget what he had said two minutes earlier.

'We've nothing but trouble with dogs,' the cashier said. 'They're in and out every minute. They get at the bars of candy. But I can't ever remember trouble with your dog.'

'He's on a leash,' said Bundy.

'That's what I'm saying,' she replied.

When Bundy came out of the store, the dog was lying down, but he made the effort to push up and sit.

'Look at you,' Bundy said, and stooped to dust him off. The way he licked himself, he picked up dirt like a blotter. A shadow moved over them, and Bundy glanced up to see, at a respectful distance, a lady beaming on the dog like a healing heat lamp. Older than Bundy – much older, a wraithlike creature, more spirit than substance, her face crossed with wisps of hair like cobwebs – Mrs Poole had known the dog as a pup; she had been a dear friend of its former owner, Miss Tyler, who had lived directly above Bundy. For years he had listened to his neighbour tease the dog to bark for pieces of liver, and heard the animal push his food dish around the kitchen.

'What ever will become of him?' Miss Tyler would whisper to Bundy, anxious that the dog shouldn't hear what she was saying. Bundy had tried to reassure her: look how spry she was at eighty! Look how the dog was overweight and asthmatic! But to ease her mind he had agreed to provide him with a home, if worst came to worst, as it did soon enough. So Bundy inherited the dog, three cases of dog food, balls and rubber bones in which the animal took no interest, along with an elegant cushioned sleeping basket he never used.

Actually, Bundy had never liked biggish dogs with very short pelts. Too much of everything, to his taste, was overexposed. The dog's long muzzle and small beady eyes put him in mind of something less than a dog. In the years with Miss Tyler, without provocation the animal would snarl at Bundy when they met on the stairs, or bark wildly when he opened his mailbox. The dog's one redeeming feature was that when he heard someone pronounce the word *sit* he would sit. That fact brought Bundy a certain distinction, and the gratitude of many shop owners. Bundy had once been a cat man.

The lingering smell of cats in his apartment had led the dog to sneeze at most of the things he sniffed.

Two men, seated on stools in the corner tavern, had turned from the bar to gaze out into the sunlight. One of them was a clerk at the supermarket where Bundy bought his dog food. 'Did he like it?' he called as Bundy came into view.

'Not particularly,' Bundy replied. Without exception, the dog did not like anything he saw advertised on television. To that extent he was smarter than Bundy, who was partial to anything served with gravy.

The open doors of the bar looked out on the intersection, when an elderly woman, as if emerging from a package, unfolded her limbs through the door of a taxi. Sheets of plate glass on a passing truck reflected Bundy and the notice that was posted in the window of the bar, advising of a change of ownership. The former owner, an Irishman named Curran, had not been popular with the new crowd of wine and beer drinkers. Nor had he been popular with Bundy. A scornful man, Curran dipped the dirty glasses in tepid water, and poured drops of sherry back into the bottles. Two epidemics of hepatitis had been traced to him. Only when he was gone did Bundy realize how much the world had shrunk. To Curran, Bundy had confessed that he felt he was now living in another country. Even more he missed Curran's favourite expression, 'Outlive the bastards!'

Two elderly men, indifferent to the screech of braking traffic, tottered toward each other to embrace near the centre of the street. One was wearing shorts. A third party, a younger woman, escorted them both to the curb. Observing an incident like this, Bundy might stand for several minutes as if he had witnessed something unusual. Under an awning, where the pair had been led, they shared the space with a woman whose gaze seemed to focus on infinity, several issues of the *Watchtower* gripped in her trembling hands.

At the corner of Sycamore and Poe streets – trees crossed poets, as a rule, at right angles – Bundy left the choice of the route up to the dog. Where the sidewalk narrowed, at the bend in the street, both man and dog prepared themselves for brief and unpredictable

Watchtower: the magazine of the Jehovah's Witnesses sect.

encounters. In the cities, people met and passed like sleepwalkers, or stared brazenly at each other, but along the sidewalks of small towns they felt the burden of their shared existence. To avoid rudeness, a lift of the eyes or a muttered greeting was necessary. This was often an annoyance for Bundy: the long approach by sidewalk, the absence of cover, the unavoidable moment of confrontation, then Bundy's abrupt greeting or a wag of his head, which occasionally startled the other person. To the young a quick 'Hi!' was appropriate, but it was not at all suitable for elderly ladies, a few with pets as escorts. To avoid these encounters, Bundy might suddenly veer into the street or an alleyway, dragging the reluctant dog behind him. He liked to meet strangers, especially children, who would pause to stroke his bald spot. What kind of dog was he? Bundy was tactfully evasive; it had proved to be an unfruitful topic. He was equally noncommittal about the dog's ineffable name.

'Call him Sport,' he would say, but this pleasantry was not appreciated. A smart aleck's answer. Their sympathies were with the dog.

To delay what lay up ahead, whatever it was, they paused at the barnlike entrance of the local van-and-storage warehouse. The draft from inside smelled of burlap sacks full of fragrant pine kindling, and mattresses that were stored on boards above the rafters. The pair contemplated a barn full of junk being sold as antiques. Bundy's eyes grazed over familiar treasure and stopped at a Morris chair with faded green corduroy cushions cradling a carton marked 'FREE KITTENS'.

He did not approach to look. One thing having a dog had spared him was the torment of losing another cat. Music (surely Elgar, something awful!) from a facsimile edition of an Atwater Kent table-model radio bathed dressers and chairs, sofas, beds and love seats, man and dog impartially. As it ended the announcer suggested that Bundy stay tuned for a Musicdote.

Recently, in this very spot – as he sniffed similar air, having paused to take shelter from a drizzle – the revelation had come to Bundy that he no longer wanted other people's junk. Better yet (or was it worse?), he no longer *wanted* – with the possible exception of an English mint, difficult to find, described as curiously strong. He

---

Musicdote: an invented word, imitating *anecdote*. A radio programme with stories or anecdotes linked to pieces of music.

had a roof, a chair, a bed, and, through no fault of his own, he had a dog. What little he had assembled and hoarded (in the garage a German electric-train set with four locomotives, and three elegant humidors and a pouch of old pipes) would soon be gratifying the wants of others. Anything else of value? The cushioned sleeping basket from Abercrombie & Fitch that had come with the dog. That would sell first. Also two Italian raincoats in good condition, and a Borsalino hat – *Extra Extra Superiore* – bought from G. Colpo in Venice.

Two young women, in the rags of fashion but radiant and blooming as gift-packed fruit, brushed Bundy as they passed, the spoor of their perfume lingering. In the flush of this encounter, his freedom from want dismantled, he moved too fast, and the leash reined him in. Rather than be rushed, the dog had stopped to sniff a meter. He found meters more life-enhancing than trees now. It had not always been so: some years ago he would tug Bundy up the incline to the park, panting and hoarsely gagging, an object of compassionate glances from elderly women headed down the grade, carrying lapdogs. This period had come to a dramatic conclusion.

In the park, back in the deep shade of the redwoods, Bundy and the dog had had a confrontation. An old tree with exposed roots had suddenly attracted the dog's attention. Bundy could not restrain him. A stream of dirt flew out between his legs to splatter Bundy's raincoat and fall into his shoes. There was something manic in the dog's excitement. In a few moments, he had frantically excavated a hole into which he could insert his head and shoulders. Bundy's tug on the leash had no effect on him. The sight of his soiled hairless bottom, his legs mechanically pumping, encouraged Bundy to give him a smart crack with the end of the leash. Not hard, but sharply, right on the button, and before he could move the dog had wheeled and the front end was barking at him savagely, the lips curled back. Dirt from the hole partially screened his muzzle, and he looked to Bundy like a maddened rodent. He was no longer a dog but some primitive, underground creature. Bundy lashed out at him, backing away, but they were joined by the leash. Unintentionally, Bundy stepped on the leash, which held the dog's snarling head to the ground. His slobbering jowls were bloody; the small veiled eyes peered up at him with hatred. Bundy had just enough presence of mind to stand there, unmoving, until they both grew calm.

Nobody had observed them. The children played and shrieked in the schoolyard as usual. The dog relaxed and lay flat on the ground, his tongue lolling in the dirt. Bundy breathed noisily, a film of perspiration cooling his face. When he stepped off the leash the dog did not move but continued to watch him warily, with bloodshot eyes. A slow burn of shame flushed Bundy's ears and cheeks, but he was reluctant to admit it. Another dog passed near them, but what he sniffed on the air kept him at a distance. In a tone of truce, if not reconciliation, Bundy said, 'You had enough?'

When had he last said that? Seated on a school chum, whose face was red with Bundy's nosebleed. He bled too easily, but the boy beneath him had had enough.

'O.K.?' he said to the dog. The faintest tremor of acknowledgement stirred the dog's tail. He got to his feet, sneezed repeatedly, then splatted Bundy with dirt as he shook himself. Side by side, the leash slack between them, they left the park and walked down the grade. Bundy had never again struck the dog, nor had the dog ever again wheeled to snarl at him. Once the leash was snapped to the dog's collar a truce prevailed between them. In the apartment he had the floor of a closet all to himself.

At the Fixit Shop on the corner of Poplar, recently refaced with green asbestos shingles, Mr Waller, the Fixit man, rapped on the glass with his wooden ruler. Both Bundy and the dog acknowledged his greeting. Waller had two cats, one asleep in the window, and a dog that liked to ride in his pickup. The two dogs had once been friends; they mauled each other a bit and horsed around like a couple of kids. Then suddenly it was over. Waller's dog would no longer trouble to leave the seat of the truck. Bundy had been so struck by this he had mentioned it to Waller. 'Hell,' Waller had said, 'Gyp's a young dog. Your dog is old.'

His saying that had shocked Bundy. There was the personal element, for one thing: Bundy was a good ten years older than Waller, and was he to read the remark to mean that Waller would soon ignore him? And were dogs – reasonably well-bred, sensible chaps – so indifferent to the facts of a dog's life? They appeared to be. One by one, as Bundy's dog grew older, the younger ones ignored him. He might have been a stuffed animal leashed to a parking meter. The human parallel was too disturbing for Bundy to dwell on it.

Old men, in particular, were increasingly touchy if they confronted Bundy at the frozen-food lockers. Did they think he was spying on them? Did they think he looked *sharper* than they did? Elderly women, as a rule, were less suspicious, and grateful to exchange a bit of chitchat. Bundy found them more realistic: they knew they were mortal. To find Bundy still around, squeezing the avocados, piqued the old men who returned from their vacations. On the other hand, Dr Biddle, a retired dentist with a glistening head like an egg in a basket of excelsior, would unfailingly greet Bundy with the words 'I'm really going to miss that mutt, you know that?' but his glance betrayed that he feared Bundy would check out first.

Bundy and the dog used the underpass walkway to cross to the supermarket parking area. Banners were flying to celebrate Whole Grains Cereal Week. In the old days, Bundy would leash the dog to a cart and they would proceed to do their shopping together, but now he had to be parked out front tied up to one of the bicycle racks. The dog didn't like it. The area was shaded and the cement was cold. Did he ever sense, however dimly, that Bundy too felt the chill? His hand brushed the coarse pelt as he fastened the leash.

'How about a new flea collar?' Bundy said, but the dog was not responsive. He sat, without being told to sit. Did it flatter the dog to leash him? Whatever Bundy would do if worst came to worst he had pondered, but had discussed with no one – his intent might be misconstrued. Of which one of them was he speaking? Impersonally appraised, in terms of survival the two of them were pretty much at a standoff: the dog was better fleshed out, but Bundy was the heartier eater.

Thinking of eating – of garlic-scented breadsticks, to be specific, dry but not dusty to the palate – Bundy entered the market to face a large display of odourless flowers and plants. The amplitude and bounty of the new market, at the point of entrance, before he selected a cart, always marked the high point of his expectations. Where

excelsior: shavings of soft wood for packing.

else in the hungry world such a prospect? Barrels and baskets of wine, six-packs of beer and bran muffins, still-warm sourdough bread that he would break and gnaw on as he shopped. Was this a cunning regression? As a child he had craved raw sugar cookies. But his euphoria sagged at the meat counter, as he studied the grey matter being sold as meat-loaf mix; it declined further at the dairy counter, where two cartons of yogurt had been sampled, and the low-fat cottage cheese was two days older than dated. By the time he entered the checkout lane, hemmed in by scandal sheets and romantic novels, the cashier's cheerfully inane 'Have a good day!' would send him off forgetting his change in the machine. The girl who pursued him (always with pennies!) had been coached to say 'Thank you, sir!'

A special on avocados this week required that Bundy make a careful selection. Out in front, as usual, dogs were barking. On the airwaves, from the rear and side, the 'Wang Wang Blues'. Why wang wang? he wondered. Besides wang wang, how did it go? The music was interrupted by an announcement on the public-address system. Would the owner of the white dog leashed to the bike rack please come to the front? Was Bundy's dog white? The point was debatable. Nevertheless, he left his cart by the avocados and followed the vegetable display to the front. People were huddled to the right of the door. A clerk beckoned to Bundy through the window. Still leashed to the bike rack, the dog lay out on his side, as if sleeping. In the parking lot several dogs were yelping.

'I'm afraid he's a goner,' said the clerk. 'These other dogs rushed him. Scared him to death. He just keeled over before they got to him.' The dog had pulled the leash taut, but there was no sign that anything had touched him. A small woman with a shopping cart thumped into Bundy.

'Is it Tiger?' she said. 'I hope it's not Tiger.' She stopped to see that it was not Tiger. 'Whose dog was it?' she asked, peering around her. The clerk indicated Bundy. 'Poor thing,' she said. 'What was his name?'

bran muffins: a bun made with bran and eaten hot, with butter. Americans eat a lot of muffins, especially at breakfast time.
sourdough bread: bread made with a raising agent other than yeast, possibly bicarbonate of soda. This kind of bread was much associated with Alaska where trappers away from civilization for months needed easy ways of making bread in camp. Sometimes such veterans of Alaska are known as *sourdoughs*.

Just recently, watching the Royal Wedding, Bundy had noticed that his emotions were nearer the surface: on two occasions his eyes had filmed over. He didn't like the woman's speaking of the dog in the past tense. Did she think he had lost his name with his life?

'What was the poor thing's name?' she repeated.

Was the tremor in Bundy's limbs noticeable? 'Victor,' Bundy lied, since he could not bring himself to admit the dog's name was Victrola. It had always been a sore point, the dog being too old to be given a new one. Miss Tyler had felt that as a puppy he looked like the picture of the dog at the horn of the gramophone. The resemblance was feeble, at best. How could a person give a dog such a name?

'Let him sit,' a voice said. A space was cleared on a bench for Bundy to sit, but at the sound of the word he could not bend his knees. He remained standing, gazing through the bright glare at the beacon revolving on the police car. One of those women who buy two frozen dinners and then go off with the shopping cart and leave it somewhere let the policeman at the crosswalk chaperon her across the street.

JOYCE CAROL OATES

Small Avalanches

Joyce Carol Oates is a novelist and a university teacher of English and comes from New York State.

The story is set in the West, in Colorado where the land is rising towards the Rocky Mountains. The story is told by a thirteen-year-old girl, still a child but changing, learning about the world. And the world could be dangerous, even close to uncle's garage.

I kept bothering my mother for a dime, so she gave me a dime, and I went down our lane and took the shortcut to the highway, and down to the gas station. My uncle Winfield ran the gas station. There were two machines in the garage and I had to decide between them: the pop machine and the candy bar machine. No, there were three machines, but the other one sold cigarettes and I didn't care about that.

It took me a few minutes to make up my mind, then I bought a bottle of Pepsi-Cola.

Sometimes a man came to unlock the machines and take out the coins, and if I happened to be there it was interesting – the way the machines could be changed so fast if you just had the right key to open them. This man drove up in a white truck with a licence plate from Kansas, a different colour from our licence plates, and he unlocked the machines and took out the money and loaded the machines up again. When we were younger we liked to hang around and watch. There was something strange about it, how the look of the machines

dime: ten cents, a tenth of a dollar.
gas station: petrol station.

could be changed so fast, the fronts swinging open, the insides show-ing, just because a man with the right keys drove up.

I went out front where my uncle was working on a car. He was under the car, lying on a thing made out of wood that had rollers on it so that he could roll himself under the car; I could just see his feet. He had on big heavy shoes that were all greasy. I asked him if my cousin Georgia was home – they lived about two miles away and I could walk – and he said no, she was baby-sitting in Stratton for three days. I already knew this but I hoped the people might have changed their minds.

'Is that man coming today to take out the money?'

My uncle didn't hear me. I was sucking at the Pepsi-Cola and running my tongue around the rim of the bottle. I always loved the taste of pop, the first two or three swallows. Then I would feel a little filled up and would have to drink it slowly. Sometimes I even poured the last of it out, but not so that anyone saw me.

'That man who takes care of the machines, is he coming today?'

'Who? No. Sometime next week.'

My uncle pushed himself out from under the car. He was my mother's brother, a few years older than my mother. He had bushy brown hair and his face was dirty. 'Did you call Georgia last night?'

'No. Ma wouldn't let me.'

'Well, somebody was on the line because Betty wanted to check on her and the goddam line was busy all night. So Betty wanted to drive in, all the way to Stratton, drive six miles when probably nothing's wrong. You didn't call her, huh?'

'No.'

'This morning Betty called her and gave her hell and she tried to say she hadn't been talking all night, that the telephone lines must have gotten mixed up. Georgia is a goddam little liar and if I catch her fooling around . . .'

He was walking away, into the garage. In the back pocket of his overalls was a dirty rag, stuffed there. He always yanked it out and wiped his face with it, not looking at it, even if it was dirty. I watched to see if he would do this and he did.

I almost laughed at this, and at how Georgia got away with mur-der. I had a good idea who was talking to her on the telephone.

The pop made my tongue tingle, a strong acid-sweet taste that almost hurt. I sat down and looked out at the road. This was in the middle of Colorado, on the road that goes through, east and west. It was a hot day. I drank one, two, three, four small swallows of pop. I pressed the bottle against my knees because I was hot. I tried to balance the bottle on one knee and it fell right over; I watched the pop trickle out onto the concrete.

I was too lazy to move my feet, so my bare toes got wet.

Somebody came along the road in a pickup truck, Mr Watkins, and he tapped on the horn to say hello to me and my uncle. He was on his way to Stratton. I thought, *Damn it, I could have hitched a ride with him.* I don't know why I bothered to think this because I had to get home pretty soon, anyway, my mother would kill me if I went to town without telling her. Georgia and I did that once, back just after school let out in June, we went down the road a ways and hitched a ride with some guy in a beat-up car we thought looked familiar, but when he stopped to let us in we didn't know him and it was too late. But nothing happened, he was all right. We walked all the way back home again because we were scared to hitch another ride. My parents didn't find out, or Georgia's, but we didn't try it again.

I followed my uncle into the gas station. The building was made of ordinary wood, painted white a few years ago but starting to peel. It was just one room. The floor was concrete, all stained with grease and cracked. I knew the whole place by heart: the ceiling planks, the black rubber things hanging on the wall, looped over big rusty spikes, the Cat's Paw ad that I liked, and the other ads for beer and cigarettes on shiny pieces of cardboard that stood up. To see those things you wouldn't guess how they came all flat, and you could unfold them and fix them yourself, like fancy things for under the Christmas tree. Inside the candy machine, behind the little windows, the candy bars stood up on display: *Milky Way, O Henry, Junior Mints, Mallow Cup, Three Musketeers, Hershey.* I liked them all. Sometimes *Milky Way* was my favourite, other times I only bought *Mallow Cup* for weeks in a row, trying to get enough of the cardboard letters to spell out *Mallow Cup.* One letter came with each candy bar, and if you spelled out the whole name you could send away for a prize. But the letter 'w' was hard to find. There were lots of 'l's', it was rotten luck to open the wrapper up and see another when you already had ten of them.

'Could I borrow a nickel?' I asked my uncle.

'I don't have any change.'

Like hell, I thought. My uncle was always stingy.

I pressed the 'return coin' knob but nothing came out. I pulled the knob out under *Mallow Cup* but nothing came out.

'Nancy, don't fool around with that thing, okay?'

'I don't have anything to do.'

'Yeah, well, your mother can find something for you to do.'

'She can do it herself.'

'You want me to tell her that?'

'Go right ahead.'

'Hey, did your father find out any more about that guy in Polo?'

'What guy?'

'Oh, I don't know, some guy who got into a fight and was arrested – he was in the Navy with your father, I don't remember his name.'

'I don't know.'

My uncle yawned. I followed him back outside and he stretched his arms and yawned. It was very hot. You could see the fake water puddles on the highway that were so mysterious and always moved back when you approached them. They could hypnotize you. Across from the garage was the mailbox on a post and then just scrub land, nothing to look at, pasture land and big rocky hills.

I thought about going to check to see if my uncle had any mail, but I knew there wouldn't be anything inside. We only got a booklet in the mail that morning, some information about how to make money selling jewellery door-to-door that I had written away for, but now I didn't care about. 'Georgia has all the luck,' I said. 'I could use a few dollars myself.'

'Yeah,' my uncle said. He wasn't listening.

I looked at myself in the outside mirror of the car he was fixing. I don't know what kind of car it was, I never memorized the makes like the boys did. It was a dark maroon colour with big heavy fenders and a bumper that had little bits of rust in it, like sparks. The running board had old, dried mud packed down inside its ruts. It was covered with black rubber, a mat. My hair was blown-looking. It was a big heavy mane of hair the colour everybody called dishwater blonde. My baby pictures showed that it used to be light blonde.

'I wish I could get a job like Georgia,' I said.

'Georgia's a year older than you.'

'Oh hell . . .'

I was thirteen but I was Georgia's size, all over, and I was smarter. We looked alike. We both had long bushy flyaway hair that frizzed up when the air was wet, but kept curls in very well when we set it, like for church. I forgot about my hair and leaned closer to the mirror to look at my face. I made my lips shape a little circle, noticing how wrinkled they got. They could wrinkle up into a small space. I poked the tip of my tongue out.

There was the noise of something on gravel, and I looked around to see a man driving in. Out by the highway my uncle just had gravel, then around the gas pumps he had concrete. This man's car was white, a colour you don't see much, and his licence plate was from Kansas.

He told my uncle to fill up the gas tank and he got out of the car, stretching his arms.

He looked at me and smiled. 'Hi,' he said.

'Hi.'

He said something to my uncle about how hot it was, and my uncle said it wasn't too bad. Because that's the way he is – always contradicting you. My mother hates him for this. But then he said, 'You read about the dry spell coming up? – right into September?' My uncle meant the ranch bureau thing but the man didn't know what he was talking about. He meant the 'Bureau News & Forecast'. This made me mad, that my uncle was so stupid, thinking that a man from out of state and probably from a city would know about that, or give a damn. It made me mad. I saw my pop bottle where it fell and I decided to go home, not to bother putting it in the case where you were supposed to.

I walked along on the edge of the road, on the pavement, because there were stones and prickles and weeds with bugs in them off the side that I didn't like to walk in barefoot. I felt hot and mad about something. A yawn started in me, and I felt it coming up like a little bubble of gas from the pop. There was my cousin Georgia in town, and all she had to do was watch a little girl who wore thick glasses and was sort of strange, but very nice and quiet and no trouble, and she'd get two dollars. I thought angrily that if anybody came along I'd put out my thumb and hitch a ride to Stratton, and the hell with my mother.

Then I did hear a car coming but I just got over to the side and waited for him to pass. I felt stubborn and wouldn't look around to see who it was, but then the car didn't pass and I looked over my shoulder – it was the man in the white car, who had stopped for gas. He was driving very slow. I got farther off the road and waited for him to pass. But he leaned over to this side and said out the open window, 'You want a ride home? Get in.'

'No, that's okay,' I said.

'Come on, I'll drive you home. No trouble.'

'No, it's okay. I'm almost home,' I said.

I was embarrassed and didn't want to look at him. People didn't do this, a grown-up man in a car wouldn't bother to do this. Either you hitched for a ride or you didn't, and if you didn't, people would never slow down to ask you. This guy is crazy, I thought. I felt very strange. I tried to look over into the field but there wasn't anything to look at, not even any cattle, just land and scrubby trees and a barbed-wire fence half falling down.

'Your feet will get all sore, walking like that,' the man said.

'I'm okay.'

'Hey, watch out for the snake!'

There wasn't any snake and I made a noise like a laugh to show that I knew it was a joke but didn't think it was very funny.

'Aren't there rattlesnakes around here? Rattlers?'

'Oh I don't know,' I said.

He was still driving right alongside me, very slow. You are not used to seeing a car slowed-down like that, it seems very strange. I tried not to look at the man. But there was nothing else to look at, just the country and the road and the mountains in the distance and some clouds.

'That man at the gas station was mad, he picked up the bottle you left.'

I tried to keep my lips pursed shut, but they were dry and came open again. I wondered if my teeth were too big in front.

'How come you walked away so fast? That wasn't friendly,' the man said. 'You forgot your pop bottle and the man back there said somebody could drive over it and get a flat tyre, he was a little mad.'

'He's my uncle,' I said.

'What?'

He couldn't hear or was pretending he couldn't hear, so I had to turn toward him. He was all-right-looking, he was smiling. 'He's my uncle,' I said.

'Oh, is he? You don't look anything like *him*. Is your home nearby?'

'Up ahead.' I was embarrassed and started to laugh, I don't know why.

'I don't see any house there,'

'You can't see it from here,' I said, laughing.

'What's so funny? My face? You know, when you smile you're a very pretty girl. You should smile all the time . . .' He was paying so much attention to me it made me laugh. 'Yes, that's a fact. Why are you blushing?'

I blushed fast, like my mother; we both hated to blush and hated people to tease us. But I couldn't get mad.

'I'm worried about your feet and the rattlers around here. Aren't there rattlers around here?'

'Oh I don't know.'

'Where I come from there are streets and sidewalks and no snakes, of course, but it isn't interesting. It isn't dangerous. I think I'd like to live here, even with the snakes – this is very beautiful, hard country, isn't it? Do you like the mountains way over there? Or don't you notice them?'

I didn't pay any attention to where he was pointing, I looked at him and saw that he was smiling. He was my father's age but he wasn't stern like my father, who had a line between his eyebrows like a knife-cut, from frowning. This man was wearing a shirt, a regular white shirt, out in the country. His hair was dampened and combed back from his forehead; it was damp right now, as if he had just combed it.

'Yes, I'd like to take a walk out here and get some exercise,' he said. His voice sounded very cheerful. 'Snakes or no snakes! You turned me down for a free ride so maybe I'll join you in a walk.'

That really made me laugh: *join you in a walk.*

'Hey, what's so funny?' he said, laughing himself.

People didn't talk like that, but I didn't say anything. He parked the car on the shoulder of the road and got out and I heard him drop the car keys in his pocket. He was scratching at his jaw. 'Well, excellent! This is excellent, healthy, divine country air! Do you like living out here?'

I shook my head, no.

'You wouldn't want to give all this up for a city, would you?'

'Sure. Any day.'

I was walking fast to keep ahead of him, I couldn't help but giggle, I was so embarrassed – this man in a white shirt was really walking out on the highway, he was really going to leave his car parked like that! You never saw a car parked on the road around here, unless it was by the creek, fishermen's cars, or unless it was a wreck. All this made my face get hotter.

He walked fast to catch up with me. I could hear coins and things jingling in his pockets.

'You never told me your name,' he said. 'That isn't friendly.'

'It's Nancy.'

'Nancy what?'

'Oh I don't know,' I laughed.

'Nancy I-Don't-Know?' he said.

I didn't get this. He was smiling hard. He was shorter than my father and now that he was out in the bright sun I could see he was older. His face wasn't tanned, and his mouth kept going into a soft smile. Men like my father and my uncles and other men never bothered to smile like that at me, they never bothered to look at me at all. Some men did, once in a while, in Stratton, strangers waiting for Greyhound buses to Denver or Kansas City, but they weren't friendly like this, they didn't keep on smiling for so long.

When I came to the path I said, 'Well, good-bye, I'm going to cut over this way. This is a shortcut.'

'A shortcut where?'

'Oh I don't know,' I said, embarrassed.

'To your house, Nancy?'

'Yeah. No, it's to our lane, our lane is half a mile long.'

'Is it? That's very long . . .'

He came closer. 'Well, good-bye,' I said.

'That's a long lane, isn't it? – it must get blocked up with snow in the winter, doesn't it? You people get a lot of snow out here –'

'Yeah.'

'So your house must be way back there . . .?' he said, pointing. He was smiling. When he stood straight like this, looking over my head, he was more like the other men. But then he looked down at me and smiled again, so friendly. I waved good-bye and jumped over the ditch and climbed the fence, clumsy as hell just when somebody was watching me, wouldn't you know it. Some barbed wire caught at my shorts and the man said, 'Let me get that loose –' but I jerked away and jumped down again. I waved good-bye again and started up the path. But the man said something and when I looked back he was climbing over the fence himself. I was so surprised that I just stood there.

'I like shortcuts and secret paths,' he said. 'I'll walk a little way with you.'

'What do you –' I started to say. I stopped smiling because something was wrong. I looked around and there was just the path behind me that the kids always took, and some boulders and old dried-up manure from cattle, and some scrubby bushes. At the top of the hill was the big tree that had been struck by lightning so many times. I was looking at all this and couldn't figure out why I was looking at it.

'You're a brave little girl to go around barefoot,' the man said, right next to me. 'Or are your feet tough on the bottom?'

I didn't know what he was talking about because I was worried; then I heard his question and said vaguely, 'I'm all right,' and started to walk faster. I felt a tingling all through me like the tingling from the Pepsi-Cola in my mouth.

'Do you always walk so fast?' the man laughed.

'Oh I don't know.'

'Is that all you can say? Nancy I-Don't-Know! That's a funny name – is it foreign?'

This made me start to laugh again. I was walking fast, then I began to run a few steps. Right away I was out of breath. That was strange – I was out of breath right away.

'Hey, Nancy, where are you going?' the man cried.

But I kept running, not fast. I ran a few steps and looked back and there he was, smiling and panting, and I happened to see his foot come down on a loose rock. I knew what would happen – the rock rolled off sideways and he almost fell, and I laughed. He glanced up at me with a surprised grin. 'This path is a booby trap, huh? Nancy has all sorts of little traps and tricks for me, huh?'

I didn't know what he was talking about. I ran up the side of the hill, careful not to step on the manure or anything sharp, and I was still out of breath but my legs felt good. They felt as if they wanted to run a long distance. 'You're going off the path,' he said, pretending to be mad. 'Hey. That's against the rules. Is that another trick?'

I giggled but couldn't think of any answer.

'Did you make this path up by yourself?' the man asked. But he was breathing hard from the hill. He stared at me, climbing up, with his hands pushing on his knees as if to help him climb. 'Little Nancy, you're like a wild colt or a deer, you're so graceful – is this your own private secret path? Or do other people use it?'

'Oh, my brother and some other kids, when they're around,' I said vaguely. I was walking backward up the hill now, so that I could look down at him. The top of his hair was thin, you could see the scalp. The very top of his forehead seemed to have two bumps, not big ones, but as if the bone went out a little, and this part was a bright pink, sunburned, but the rest of his face and his scalp were white.

He stepped on another loose rock, and the rock and some stones and mud came loose. He fell hard on to his knee. 'Jesus!' he said. The way he stayed down like that looked funny. I had to press my hand over my mouth. When he looked up at me his smile was different. He got up, pushing himself up with his hands, grunting, and then he wiped his hands on his trousers. The dust showed on them. He looked funny.

'Is my face amusing? Is it a good joke?'

I didn't mean to laugh, but now I couldn't stop. I pressed my hand over my mouth hard.

He stared at me. 'What do you see in my face, Nancy? What do you see – anything? Do you see my soul, do you see *me*, is that what you're laughing at?' He took a fast step toward me, but I jumped back. It was like a game. 'Come on, Nancy, slow down, just slow down,' he said. 'Come on, Nancy . . .'

I didn't know what he was talking about, I just had to laugh at his face. It was so tense and strange; it was so *important*.

I noticed a big rock higher up, and I went around behind it and pushed it loose – it rolled right down toward him and he had to scramble to get out of the way. 'Hey! Jesus!' he yelled. The rock came loose with some other things and a mud chunk got him in the leg.

I laughed so hard my stomach started to ache.

He laughed too, but a little different from before.

'This is a little trial for me, isn't it?' he said. 'A little preliminary contest. Is that how the game goes? Is that your game, Nancy?'

I ran higher up the hill, off to the side where it was steeper. Little rocks and things came loose and rolled back down. My breath was coming so fast it made me wonder if something was wrong. Down behind me the man was following, stooped over, looking at me, and his hand was pressed against the front of his shirt. I could see his hand moving up and down because he was breathing so hard. I could even see his tongue moving around the edge of his dried-out lips . . . I started to get afraid, and then the tingling came back into me, beginning in my tongue and going out through my whole body, and I couldn't help giggling.

He said something that sounded like, '– won't be laughing –' but I couldn't hear the rest of it. My hair was all wet in back where it would be a job for me to unsnarl it with the hairbrush. The man came closer, stumbling, and just for a joke I kicked out at him, to scare him – and he jerked backward and tried to grab onto a branch of a bush, but it slipped through his fingers and he lost his balance and fell. He grunted. He fell so hard that he just lay there for a minute. I wanted to say I was sorry, or ask him if he was all right, but I just stood there grinning.

He got up again; the fleshy part of his hand was bleeding. But he didn't seem to notice it and I turned and ran up the rest of the hill, going almost straight up the last part, my legs were so strong and felt so good. Right at the top I paused, just balanced there, and a gust of wind would have pushed me over – but I was all right. I laughed aloud, my legs felt so springy and strong.

I looked down over the side where he was crawling, down on his hands and knees again. 'You better go back to Kansas! Back home to Kansas!' I laughed. He stared up at me and I waited for him to smile again but he didn't. His face was very pale. He was staring at me but he seemed to be seeing something else, his eyes were very serious and strange. I could see his belt creasing his stomach, the bulge of his white shirt. He pressed his hand against his chest again. 'Better go home, go home, get in your damn old car and go home,' I sang, making a song of it. He looked so serious, staring up at me. I pretended to kick at him again and he flinched, his eyes going small.

'Don't leave me –' he whimpered.

'Oh go on,' I said.

'Don't leave – I'm sick – I think I –'

His face seemed to shrivel. He was drawing in his breath very slowly, carefully, as if checking to see how much it hurt, and I waited for this to turn into another joke. Then I got tired of waiting and just rested back on my heels. My smile got smaller and smaller, like his.

'Good-bye, I'm going,' I said, waving. I turned and he said something – it was like a cry – but I didn't want to bother going back. The tingling in me was almost noisy.

I walked over to the other side, and slid back down to the path and went along the path to our lane. I was very hot. I knew my face was flushed and red. 'Damn old nut,' I said. But I had to laugh at the way he had looked, the way he kept scrambling up the hill and was just crouched there at the end, on his hands and knees. He looked so funny, bent over and clutching at his chest, pretending to have a heart attack or maybe having one, a little one, for all I knew. This will teach you a lesson, I thought.

By the time I got home my face had dried off a little, but my hair was like a haystack. I stopped by the old car parked in the lane, just a junker on blocks, and looked in the outside rear-view mirror – the mirror was all twisted around because people looked in it all the time. I tried to fix my hair by rubbing my hands down hard against it, but no luck. 'Oh damn,' I said aloud, and went up the steps to the back, and remembered not to let the screen door slam so my mother wouldn't holler at me.

She was in the kitchen ironing, just sprinkling some clothes on the ironing board. She used a pop bottle painted blue and fitted out with a sprinkler top made of rubber, that I fixed for her at grade school a long time ago for a Christmas present; she shook the bottle over the clothes and stared at me. 'Where have you been? I told you to come right back.'

'I did come right back.'

'You're all dirty, you look like hell. What happened to you?'

'Oh I don't know,' I said. 'Nothing.'

She threw something at me – it was my brother's shirt – and I caught it and pressed it against my hot face.

'You get busy and finish these,' my mother said. 'It must be ninety-five in here and I'm fed up. And you do a good job, I'm really fed up. Are you listening, Nancy? Where the hell is your mind?'

I liked the way the damp shirt felt on my face. 'Oh I don't know,' I said.

FREDERIK POHL

The Fiend

Though this is a science-fiction tale (it takes place on a spaceship), it is the lonely captain's thoughts and feelings and terrors that make the action. As in the Asimov story, the past catches up. But is Dandish the fiend?

Frederik Pohl is a popular writer of science fiction and something of a satirist.

How beautiful she was, Dandish thought, and how helpless. The plastic identification ribbon around her neck stood out straight, and as she was just out of the transport capsule, she wore nothing else.

'Are you awake?' he asked, but she did not stir.

Dandish felt excitement building up inside him, she was so passive and without defence. A man could come to her now and do anything at all to her, and she would not resist. Or, of course, respond. Without touching her he knew that her body would be warm and dry. It was fully alive, and in a few minutes she would be conscious.

Dandish – who was the captain and sole crew member of the interstellar ship without a name, carrying congealed colonists across the long, slow, empty space from Earth to a planet that circled a star that had never had a name in astronomical charts, only a number, and was now called Eleanor – passed those minutes without looking again at the girl, whose name he knew to be Silvie, but whom he had never met. When he looked again she was awake, jackknifed against the safety straps of the crib, her hair standing out around her head and her face wearing an expression of anger.

'All right. Where are you? I know what the score is,' she said. 'Do you know what they can do to you for this?'

Dandish was startled. He did not like being startled, for it frightened him. For nine years the ship had been whispering across space; he had had enough of loneliness to satisfy him and he had been frightened. There were 700 cans of colonists on the ship, but they lay brittle and changeless in their bath of liquid helium and were not very good company. Outside the ship the nearest human being was perhaps two light-years away, barring some chance-met ship heading in the other direction that was actually far more remote than either star, since the forces involved in stopping and matching course with a vessel bound home were twice as great as, and would take twice as much time as, those involved in the voyage itself.

Everything about the trip was frightening. The loneliness was a terror. To stare down through an inch of crystal and see nothing but far stars led to panic. Dandish had decided to stop looking out five years before, but had not been able to keep to his decision, and so now and again peeped, through the crystal and contemplated his horrifying visions of the seal breaking, the crystal popping out on a breath of air, himself in his metal prison tumbling, tumbling for ever down to the heart of one of the 10,000,000 stars that lay below.

In this ship a noise was an alarm. Since no one but himself was awake, to hear a scratch of metal or a thud of a moving object striking something else, however tiny, however remote, was a threat, and more than once Dandish had suffered through an itch of fear for hours or days until he tracked down the exploded light tube or unsecured door that had startled him. He dreamed uneasily of fire. This was preposterously unlikely, in the steel and crystal ship, but what he was dreaming of was not the fire of a house but the monstrous fires in the stars beneath.

'Come out where I can see you,' commanded the girl.

Dandish noted that she had not troubled to cover her nakedness. Bare she woke and bare she stayed. She had unhitched the restraining webbing and left the crib, and now she was prowling the room in which she had awakened, looking for him.

'They warned us,' she called. ' "Watch the hook!" "Look out for the space nuts!" "You'll be sorry!" That's all we heard at the Reception Centre, and now here you are, all right. Wherever you are. Where are you? For God's sake, come out where I can see you.'

She half stood and half floated at an angle to the floor, nibbling at imperceptible bits of dead skin on her lips and staring warily from side to side. She said, 'What was the story you were going to tell me? A subspace meteorite destroyed the ship, all but you and me, and we were doomed to fly endlessly towards nowhere, so there was nothing for us to do but try to make a life for ourselves?'

Dandish watched her through the view eyes in the reviving room, but did not answer. He was a connoisseur of victims, Dandish was. He had spent a great deal of time planning this. Physically she was perfect, very young, slim, slight. He had picked her out on that basis from among the 352 female canned colonists, leafing through the microfile photographs that accompanied each colonist's dossier like a hi-fi hobbyist shopping through a catalogue. She had been the best of the lot.

Dandish was not skilled enough to read a personality profile, and in any event considered psychologists to be phonies and their profiles trash, so he had to go by the indices he knew. He had wanted his victim to be innocent and trusting. Silvie, 16 years old and a little below average intelligence, had seemed very promising. It was disappointing that she did not react with more fear.

'They'll give you fifty years for this!' she shouted, looking around to see where he could be hiding. 'You know that, don't you?'

The revival crib, sensing that she was out of it, was quietly stowing and rearming itself, ready to be taken out and used again. Its plastic sheets slipped free of the corners, rolled up in a tight spiral, and slid into a disposal chute, revealing aseptic new sheets below. Its radio-warming generators tested themselves with a surge of high-voltage current, found no flaws, and shut themselves off. The crib sides folded down meekly. The instrument table hooded itself over. The girl paused to watch it, then shook her head and laughed.

'Scared of me?' she called. 'Come on, let's get this over with! Or else,' she added, 'admit you've made a boo-boo, get me some clothes and let's talk this over sensibly.'

Sorrowfully Dandish turned his gaze away. A timing device reminded him that it was time to make his routine half-hour check of the ship's systems and, as he had done more than 150,000 times already and would do 100,000 times again, he swiftly scanned the temperature readings in the can hold, metered the loss of liquid helium and balanced it against the withdrawals from the reserve, compared the ship's course with the flight plan, measured the fuel consumption and rate of flow, found all systems functioning smoothly, and returned to the girl.

It had taken only a minute or so, but already she had found the comb and mirror he had put out for her and was working angrily at her hair. One fault in the techniques of freezing and revivification lay in what happened to such elaborated structures as fingernails and hair. At the temperature of liquid helium all organic matter was brittle and although the handling techniques were planned with that fact in mind, the body wrapped gently in elastic cocooning, every care exercised to keep it from contact with anything hard or sharp, nails and hair had a way of being snapped off. The Reception Centre endlessly drummed into the colonists the importance of short nails and butch haircuts, but the colonists were not always convinced. Silvie now looked like a dummy on which a student wigmaker had failed a test. She solved her problem at last by winding what remained of her hair in a tiny bun and put down the comb, snapped-off strands of her hair floating in the air all about her like a stretched-out sandstorm.

She patted the bun mournfully and said, 'I guess you think this is pretty funny.'

Dandish considered the question. He was not impelled to laugh. Twenty years before, when Dandish was a teenager with the long permanented hair and the lacquered fingernails that were the fashion for kids that year, he had dreamed almost every night of just such a situation as this. To own a girl of his own – not to love her or to rape her or to marry her, but to possess her as a slave, with no one anywhere to stop him from whatever he chose to impose on her – had elaborated itself in a hundred variations nightly.

He didn't tell anyone about his dream, not directly, but in the school period devoted to practical psychology he had mentioned it as something he had read in a book and the instructor, staring right through him into his dreams, told him it was a repressed wish to play with dolls. 'This fellow is role playing,' he said, 'acting out a wish to be a woman. These clear-cut cases of repressed homosexuality can take many forms . . .' and on and on, and although the dreams were as physically satisfying as ever, the young Dandish awoke from them both reproved and resentful.

But Silvie was neither a dream nor a doll. 'I'm not a doll,' said

Silvie, so sharply and patly that it was a shock. 'Come on out and get it over with!'

She straightened up, holding to a free-fall grip, and although she looked angry and annoyed she still did not seem afraid. 'Unless you are really crazy,' she said clearly, 'which I doubt, although I have to admit it's a possibility, you aren't going to do anything I don't want you to do, you know. Because you can't get away with it, right? You can't kill me, you could never explain it, and besides they don't let murderers run ships in the first place, and so when we land all I have to do is yell cop and you're running a subway shuttle for the next ninety years.' She giggled. 'I know about that. My uncle got busted on income-tax evasion and now he's a self-propelled dredge in the Amazon delta, and you should see the letters he writes. So come on out and let's see what I'm willing to let you get away with.'

She grew impatient. 'Kee-rist,' she said, shaking her head. 'I sure get the great ones. And, oh, by the way, as long as I'm up, I have to go to the little girls' room, and then I want breakfast.'

Dandish took some small satisfaction in that these requirements, at least, he had foreseen. He opened the door to the washroom and turned on the warmer oven where emergency rations were waiting. By the time Silvie came back biscuits, bacon, and hot coffee were set out for her.

'I don't suppose you have a cigarette?' she asked. 'Well, I'll live. How about some clothes? And how about coming out so I can get a look at you?' She stretched and yawned and then began to eat.

Apparently she had showered, as was generally desirable on awakening from freeze-sleep to get rid of the exfoliated skin, and she had wrapped her ruined hair in a small towel. Dandish had left one small towel in the washroom, reluctantly, but it had not occurred to him that his victim would wrap it around her head. Silvie sat thoughtfully staring at the remains of her breakfast and then after a while said, like a lecturer:

'As I understand it, starship sailors are always some kind of nut, because who else would go off for twenty years at a time, even for money, even for any kind of money? All right, you're a nut. So if you wake me up and won't come out, won't talk to me, there's nothing I can do about it.

'Now, I can see that even if you weren't a little loopy to start with, this kind of life would tip you. Maybe you just want a little company? I can understand that. I might even co-operate and say no more about it.

'On the other hand, maybe you're trying to get your nerve up for something rough. Don't know if you can, because they naturally screened you down fine before they gave you the job. But supposing. What happens then?

'If you kill me, they catch you.

'If you don't kill me, then I'll tell them when we land, and they catch you.

'I told you about my uncle. Right now his body is in the deep-freeze somewhere on the dark side of Mercury and they've got his brain keeping the navigation channels clear off Belem. Maybe you think that's not so bad. Uncle Henry doesn't like it a bit. He doesn't have any company, bad as you that way, I guess, and he says his suction hoses are always sore. Of course he could always louse up on the job, but then they'd just put him some other place that wouldn't be quite as nice – so what he does is grit his teeth, or I guess you should say his grinders, and get along the best he can. Ninety years! He's only done six so far. I mean six when I left Earth, whatever that is now. You wouldn't like that. So why not come out and talk?'

Five or ten minutes later, after making faces and buttering another roll and flinging it furiously at the wall, where the disposal units sluiced it away, she said, 'Damn you, then give me a book to read, anyway.'

Dandish retreated from her and listened to the whisper of the ship for a few minutes, then activated the mechanisms of the revival crib. He had been a loser long enough to learn when to cut his losses. The girl sprang to her feet as the sides of the crib unfolded. Gentle tentacles reached out for her and deposited her in it, locking the webbing belt around her waist.

'You damned fool!' she shouted, but Dandish did not answer.

The anaesthesia cone descended towards her struggling face, and she screamed. 'Wait a minute! I never said I wouldn't –' but what she never said she wouldn't, she couldn't say, because the cone cut her off. A plastic sack stretched itself around her, moulding to her face, her body, her legs, even to the strayed towel around her hair, and the revival crib rolled silently to the freezing room.

Dandish did not watch further. He knew what would happen, and besides, the timer reminded him to make his check. Temperatures, normal; fuel consumption, normal; course, normal; freezer room showed one new capsule en route to storage, otherwise normal. Goodbye, Silvie, said Dandish to himself, you were a pretty bad mistake.

Conceivably later on, with another girl . . .

But it had taken nine years for Dandish to wake Silvie, and he did not think he could do it again. He thought of her Uncle Henry running a dredge along the South Atlantic littoral. It could have been him. He had leaped at the opportunity to spend his sentence piloting a starship instead.

He stared out at the 10,000,000 stars below with the optical receptors that were his eyes. He clawed helplessly at space with the radars that gave him touch. He wept a 5,000,000-mile stream of ions behind him from his jets. He thought of the tons of helpless flesh in his hold, the bodies in which he could have delighted, if his own body had not been with Uncle Henry's on coldside Mercury, the fears on which he could have fed, if he had been able to inspire fear. He would have sobbed, if he had had a voice to sob with.

NORMAN RUSH

Bruns

Norman Rush is another New Yorker. The narrator in this story is a woman and an anthropologist. So she is a trained observer of the South African scene. It is very much the old South Africa where Boer farmers treat their black workers almost as slaves. Bruns is not a Boer, though; he is a Dutchman with religion . . .

Poor Bruns. They hated him so much it was baroque. But then so is Keteng baroque, everything about it.

Probably the Boers were going to hate Bruns no matter what. Boers run Keteng. They've been up there for generations, since before the Protectorate. When independence came, it meant next to nothing to them. They ignored it. They're all citizens of Botswana, but they are Boers underneath forever, really unregenerate. Also, in Keteng you're very close to the border with South Africa. They still mostly use rands for money instead of pula. Boers slightly intrigue me. For a woman, I'm somewhat an elitist, and hierarchy always interests me. I admit these things. The Boers own everything in Keteng, including the chief. They wave him to the head of the queue for petrol, which he gets for free, naturally, just like the cane liquor they give him. They own the shops. Also they think they really know how to manage the Bakorwa, which actually they do. You have to realize that the Bakorwa have the reputation of being the most violent and petulant tribe in the country, which is about right. All the other tribes say so. And in fact the Boers do get along with them. In fact, the original whites in Keteng – that would be the Vissers, Du Toits, Pieterses . . . seven families altogether – were

baroque: grotesque.

all rescued by the Bakorwa when their ox wagons broke down in the desert when they were trekking somewhere. They started out as bankrupts and now they own the place. It's so feudal up there you cannot conceive. That is, it has been until now.

I know a lot about Keteng. I got interested in Keteng out of boredom with my project. Actually, my project collapsed. My thesis adviser at Stanford talked me into my topic anyway, so it wasn't all that unbearable when it flopped. At certain moments I can even get a certain vicious satisfaction out of it. Frankly, the problem is partly too many anthropologists in one small area. We are thick on the ground. And actually we hate each other. The problem is that people are contaminating one another's research, so hatred is structural and I don't need to apologize. At any rate, I was getting zero. I was supposed to be showing a relationship between diet and fertility among the Bakorwa up near Tsopong, in the hills. The theory was that fertility would show some seasonality because the diet in the deep bush was supposedly ninety per cent hunting-gathering, which would mean sharp seasonal changes in diet content. But the sad fact is you go into the middle of nowhere and people are eating Simba chips and cornflakes and drinking Castle lager. The problem is Americans, partly. Take the hartebeest domestication project, where they give away so much food and scraps and things that you have a kind of permanent beggar settlement outside the gate. And just to mention the other research people you have encumbering the ground – you have me, you have the anthropologists from the stupid Migration Study and the census, and you have people from some land-grant college someplace following baboons around. By the way, there were some baboon attacks on Bakorwa gathering firewood around Keteng, which they blame on the Americans for pestering the baboons. Or Imiricans, as the Boers would say. America gets the blame.

The other thing is that Keteng is remote. It's five hours from the rail line, over unspeakable roads, through broiling-hot empty thornveldt. In one place there's no road and you just creep over red granite swells for a kilometer, following a little line of rocks. So the Boers got used to doing what they wanted, black government or

Stanford: an American university in California, with a high reputation for scholarship.
thornveldt: poor pasture, almost scrubland.

not. They still pay their farm labour in sugar and salt and permission to crawl underneath their cows and suck fresh milk. It is baroque. So I got interested in Keteng and started weekending. At my project site, camping was getting uncomfortable, I should mention, with strange figures hanging around my perimeter. Nobody did anything, but it makes you nervous. In Keteng I can always get a room from the sisters at the mission hospital and a bath instead of washing my armpits under my shirt because you never know who's watching.

The place I stay when I descend into Keteng is interesting and is one reason I keep going back. I can see everything from the room the sisters give me. The hospital is up on the side of a hill, and the sisters' hostel is higher than that, on the very top. My room is right under the roof, the second storey, where there's a water tank and therefore a perpetual sound of water gurgling down through pipes, a sound you get famished for in a place so arid. Also, in tubs on the roof they have vines growing that drape down over the face of the building, so you have this green-curtain effect over your window. The sisters have a little tiny enclosed locked-up courtyard where they hang their underthings to dry, which is supposed to be secret and sacrosanct, which you can see into from my room. You can also see where Bruns stayed – a pathetic bare little shack near the hospital with gravel around the stoop and a camp stool so he could sit in the sun and watch his carrots wither. At the foot of the hill the one street in Keteng begins at the hospital gate and runs straight to the chief's court at the other end of town. Downtown amounts to a dozen one-storey buildings – shops – with big houses behind them. You can see the Bakorwa wards spreading away from the centre of Keteng – log kraals, mud rondavels with thatch, mostly, although cement-block square houses with sheet-metal roofs held down by cobbles are infiltrating the scene. Sometimes I think anthropology should be considered a form of voyeurism rather than a science, with all the probing into reproductive life and so forth we do. I'm voyeuristic. I like to pull my bed up to the window and lie there naked, studying Keteng. Not that the street life is so exotic. Mostly it's goats and cattle. I did once see a guy frying a piece of meat on a shovel. The nuns have really hard beds, which I happen to prefer.

Poor Bruns. The first thing I ever heard about him was that there
kraals . . . rondavels: huts.

was somebody new in Keteng who was making people as nervous as poultry, as they put it. That's an Afrikaans idiom. They meant Bruns. He was a volunteer from some Netherlands religious outfit and a conscientious objector like practically all the Dutch and German volunteers are. He was assigned to be the fleet mechanic at the mission hospital. He was a demon mechanic, it turned out, who could fix anything. Including the X-ray machine, for example, which was an old British Army World War I field unit, an antique everybody had given up on. Of course, what do the Boers care, because when they get even just a little cut it's into the Cessna and over the border into the Republic to Potgietersrust or even Pretoria. But other people were ecstatic. Bruns was truly amazing. People found out. A few of the Bakorwa farmers have tractors or old trucks, and Bruns, being hyper-Christian, of course started fixing them up for free in his spare time. On Saturdays you'd see Bakorwa pushing these old wrecks, hordes of them pushing these three or four old wrecks toward Keteng for Bruns. So, number one, right away that made Bruns less than popular around Du Toit's garage. Du Toit didn't like it. It even got a little mean, with some of Bruns's tools disappearing from his workroom at the hospital until he started really locking things up.

The other thing that fed into making people nervous right away was Bruns physically. He was very beautiful, I don't know how else to put it. He was very Aryan, with those pale-blue eyes that are apparently so de rigueur for male movie stars these days. He had a wonderful physique. At some point possibly he had been a physical culturist, or maybe it was just the effect of constant manual work and lifting. Also I can't resist mentioning a funny thing about Boer men. Or, rather, let me back into it: there is a thing with black African men called the African Physiological Stance, which means essentially that men, when they stand around, don't bother to hold their bellies in. It might seem like a funny cultural trait to borrow, but Boer men picked it up. It doesn't look so bad with blacks because the men stay pretty skinny, usually. But in whites, especially in Boers, who run to fat anyway, it isn't so enthralling. They wear their belts underneath their paunches, somewhat on the order of a sling. Now consider Bruns strictly as a specimen walking around with his nice flat belly, a real waist, and, face it, a very compact nice little behind, and also keep in mind that he's Dutch, so in a remote way he's the same stock as the Boer men there, and the contrast was not going to be lost on the women, who are another story. The women have nothing to do. Help is thick on the ground. They get up at noon. They consume bales of true-romance magazines from Britain and the Republic, so incredibly crude. They do makeup. And they can get very flirtatious in an incredibly heavy-handed way after a couple of brandies. Bruns was the opposite of flirtatious. I wonder what the women thought it meant. He was very scrupulous when he was talking to you – it was nice. He never seemed to be giving you ratings on your secondary sex characteristics when he was talking to you, unlike everybody else. He kept his eyes on your face. As a person with large breasts I'm sensitized on this. Boer men are not normal. They think they're a godsend to any white woman who turns up in this wilderness. Their sex ideas are derived from their animals. I've heard they just unbanned 'Love Without Fear' in South Africa this year, which says something. The book was published in 1941.

On top of that, the Dutch-Boer interface is so freakish and tense anyway. The Dutch call Afrikaans 'baby Dutch'. Boers are a humiliation to the Dutch, like they are their ids set free in the world or something similar. The Dutch Parliament keeps almost voting to get an oil boycott going against South Africa.

Also it wasn't helpful that Bruns was some kind of absolute vegetarian, which he combined with fasting. He was whatever is beyond lactovegetarian in strictness. You have never seen people consume meat on the scale of the Boers. As a friend of mine says, Boers and meat go together like piss and porcelain. Biltong, sausages, any kind of meat product, pieces of pure solid fat – they love meat. So there was another rub.

Bruns was so naive. He apparently had no idea he was coming to live in a shame culture. Among the Bakorwa, if you do something wrong and somebody catches you, they take you to the customary court and give you a certain number of strokes with a switch in public. They wet it first so it hurts more. This is far from being something whites thought up and imposed. It's the way it is. The

id: a word from Freudian psychology meaning instinctive impulses.
lactovegetarian: the kind of vegetarian who will eat dairy produce.
biltong: strips of sun-dried meat, originally for long journeys through rough country.

nearest regular magistrate is – where? Bobonong? Who knows? Bakorwa justice is based on beatings and the fear of beatings and shame, full stop. It's premodern. But here comes Bruns wearing his crucifix and wondering what is going on. The problem was he had an unfortunate introduction to the culture. You could call wife beating among the Bakorwa pretty routine. I think he saw an admission to the hospital related to that. Also he himself was an ex-battered child, somebody said. I'm thinking of setting up a course for people who get sent here. I can give you an example of the kind of thing people should know about and not think twice about. The manager of the butchery in one of the towns caught two women shoplifting and he made them stand against the wall while he whipped them with an extension cord instead of calling the police. This shamed them and was probably effective and they didn't lose time from work or their families. You need anthropologists to prepare people for the culture here. Bruns needed help. He needed information.

Bruns belonged to some sect. It was something like the people in England who jump out and disrupt fox hunts. Or there was a similar group, also in England, of people who were interposing themselves between prizefighters, to stop prizefighting. Bruns was from some milieu like that. I think he felt like he'd wandered into something by Hieronymus Bosch which he was supposed to do something about.

The fact is that the amount of fighting and beating there is in Bakorwa culture is fairly staggering to a person at first. Kids get beaten at school and at home, really hard sometimes. Wives naturally get beaten. Animals. Pets. Donkeys. And of course the whole traditional court process, the *kgotla*, is based on it. I think he was amazed. Every Wednesday at the *kgotla* the chief hears charges and your shirt comes off and you get two to twenty strokes, depending. Then there's the universal recreational punching and shoving that goes on when the locals start drinking. So it's not something you can afford to be sensitive about if you're going to work here for any length of time.

Bruns decided to do something. The first thing he tried was absurd and made everything worse.

He started showing up at the *kgotla* when they were giving judge-

Hieronymus Bosch: a medieval painter who painted demons.

ment and just stood there watching them give strokes. He was male, so he could get right up in the front row. I understand he never said anything, the idea being just to be a sorrowful witness. I guess he thought it would have some effect. But the Bakorwa didn't get it and didn't care. He was welcome.

Maybe I'm just a relativist on corporal punishment. Our own wonderful culture is falling apart with crime, more than Keteng is, and you could take the position that substituting imprisonment for the various kinds of rough justice there used to be has only made things worse. Who knows if there was less crime when people just formed mobs in a cooperative spirit and rode people out of town on a rail or horsewhipped them, when that was the risk you were running rather than plea bargaining and courses in basket weaving or some other fatuous kind of so-called rehabilitation? I don't.

Bruns convinced himself that the seven families were to blame for all the violence – spiritually to blame at least. He was going to ask them to do something about it, take some kind of stand, and he was going to the centre of power, Deon Du Toit.

There's some disagreement as to whether Bruns went once to Du Toit's house or twice. Everybody agrees Du Toit wasn't home and that Bruns went in and stayed, however many times he went, stayed talking with Marika, Du Toit's slutty wife. The one time everybody agrees on was at night. Bruns started to turn away when the maid told him Du Toit wasn't there. But then somehow Bruns was invited in. That's established. Then subsequently there was one long afternoon encounter, supposedly.

Bruns was going to blame the families for everything – for making money off liquor, which leads to violence, for doing nothing about violence to women and not even appearing in *kgotla* for women who worked for them when they were brutalized by their husbands or boyfriends, for corrupting the chief, who was an incompetent anyway, for doing nothing about conditions at the jail. I can generate this list out of my own knowledge of Bruns's mind: everything on it is true. Finally there was something new he was incensed about. The drought had been bad and Du Toit had just started selling water for three pula a drum. You know a drought is bad when cattle come into town and bite the brass taps off cisterns. A wildebeest charged an old woman carrying melons and knocked her down so it could get the moisture in the melons.

We know what Du Toit did when he came back and found out Bruns had been there. First he punched the housemaid, Myriad Gofetile (her twin sister also works for Du Toit), for letting Bruns in or for not telling him about it, one or the other. And Marika wasn't seen outside the house for a while, although the Boers usually try not to mark their women where it shows when they beat them.

Those are two people I would love to see fighting, Deon and Marika Du Toit, tooth and nail. It would be gorgeous. Both of them are types. He's fairly gigantic. Marika has skin like a store dummy's. She's proud of it. She's one of those people who are between twenty-five and forty but you can't tell where. She has high cheekbones you can't help envying, and these long eyes, rather Eurasian-looking. She wears her hair like a fool, though – lacquered, like a scoop around her head. Her hair is yellowish. She hardly says anything. But she doesn't need to because she's so brilliant with her cigarette, smoking and posing.

Deon was away hunting during the time or times Bruns visited. The inevitable thing happened, besides beating up on his household, when Deon found out. This was the day he got back, mid-morning. He sent a yard boy to the hospital with a message to the effect that Bruns is ordered to drop whatever he's doing and come immediately to see Deon at the house.

Bruns is cool. He sends back the message that he's engaged on work for the hospital and regrets he isn't free to visit.

So that message went back, and the yard boy comes back with a new command that Bruns should come to Du Toit's at tea, which would be at about eleven. Bruns sends the message back that he doesn't break for tea, which was true.

Suddenly you have Deon himself materializing in the hospital garage, enraged, still covered with gore from hauling game out of his pickup. He had shot some eland.

'You don't come by my wife when I am away?' He ended up screaming this at Bruns, who just carried on fixing some vehicle.

He now orders Bruns to come to his house at lunch, calling him a worm and so on, which was apropos Bruns being a pacifist.

Bruns took the position that he had authority over who was present in the garage and ordered Du Toit to leave.

Then there was a stupid exchange to the effect that Bruns would come only if Du Toit was in actual fact inviting him to a meal at noon.

Throughout all this Bruns is projecting a more and more sorrowful calmness. Also, everything Bruns says is an aside, since he keeps steadily working. Deon gets frantic. The sun is pounding down. You have this silent chorus of Africans standing around. There is no question but that they are loving every moment.

It ends with Deon telling Bruns he had better be at his house at noon if he expects to live to have sons.

Of course, after the fact everybody wanted to know why somebody didn't intervene.

Bruns did go at lunchtime to Deon's.

The whole front of Deon's place is a screened veranda he uses for making biltong. From the street it looks like red laundry. There are eight or nine clotheslines perpetually hung with rags of red meat turning purple, air-drying. This is where they met. Out in the road you had an audience of Bakorwa pretending to be going somewhere, slowly.

Meat means flies. Here is where the absurd takes a hand. Deon comes into the porch from the house. Bruns goes into the porch from the yard. The confrontation is about to begin. Deon is just filling his lungs to launch out at Bruns when the absurd thing happens: he inhales a fly. Suddenly you have a farce going. The fly apparently got rather far up his nostril. Deon goes into a fit, stamping and snorting. He's in a state of terror. You inhale a fly and the body takes over. Also you have to remember that there are certain flies that fly up the nostrils of wildebeests and lay eggs that turn into maggots that eat the brains of the animals, which makes them gallop in circles until they die of exhaustion. Deon has seen this, of course.

The scene is over before it begins. Deon crashes back into his living room screaming for help. It is total public humiliation. The Bakorwa see Bruns walk away nonchalantly and hear Du Toit thrashing and yelling.

Marika got the fly out with tweezers, I heard. By then Bruns was back at work.

Here is my theory of the last act. Deon's next move was inevitable – to arrange for a proxy to catch Bruns that same night and give him a beating. For symbolic and other reasons, it had to be one of the Bakorwa. At this point both Bruns and Deon are deep in the grip of the process of the Duel, capital D. Pragmatically, there would be no problem for Deon in getting one of the Bakorwa to do the job and probably even take the blame for it in the unlikely event he got caught. This is not to say there was no risk to Deon, because there was, some. But if you dare a Boer to do something, which is undoubtedly the way Deon perceived it, he is lost. An example is a man who was dared to kiss a rabid ox on the lips, at the abattoir in Cape Town. It was in the *Rand Daily Mail*. By the way, the point of kissing the ox on the lips is that it gives rabies its best chance of getting directly to your brain. So he did it. Not only that, he defaulted on the course of rabies injections the health department was frantically trying to get him to take. Here is your typical Boer folk hero. Add to that the Duel psychology, which is like a spell that spreads out and paralyzes people who might otherwise be expected to step in and put a stop to something so weird. Still, when someone you know personally like Bruns is found dead, it shocks you. I had cut this man's hair.

I'm positive two things happened the last night, although the official version is that only one did.

The first is that Deon sent somebody, a local, to beat Bruns up. When night falls in Keteng it's like being under a rock. There's no street lighting. The stores are closed. The whites pull their curtains. Very few Bakorwa can afford candles or paraffin lamps. It can seem unreal, because the Bakorwa are used to getting out and about in the dark and you can hear conversations and deals going down and so on, all in complete blackness. They even have parties in the dark where you can hear *bojalwa* being poured and people singing and playing those one-string tin-can violins. There was no moon that night and it was cloudy.

Bruns would often go out after dinner and sit on one of the big rocks up on the hill and do his own private vespers. He'd go out at sunset and sit there into the night thinking pure thoughts. He had a little missal he took with him, but what he could do with it in the dark except fondle it I have no idea.

So I think Bruns went out, got waylaid and beaten up as a lesson, and went back to his hut. I think the point of it was mainly just to humiliate him and mark him up. Of course, because of his beliefs, he would feel compelled just to endure the beating. He might try to shield his head or kidneys, but he couldn't fight back. He would not be in the slightest doubt that it was Bakorwa doing it and that they had been commissioned by Du Toit. So he comes back messed up, and what is he supposed to do?

Even very nice people find it hard to resist paradox. For example, whenever somebody who knows anything about it tells the story of poor Bruns, they always begin with the end of the story, which is that he drowned, their little irony being that of course everybody knows Botswana is a desert and Keteng is a desert. So poor Bruns, his whole story and what he did is reduced to getting this cheap initial sensation out of other people.

As I reconstruct the second thing that happened, it went like this: Bruns wandered back from his beating and possibly went into his place with the idea of cleaning himself up. His state of mind would have to be fairly terrible at this point. He has been abused by the very people he is trying to champion. At the same time, he knows Du Toit is responsible and that he can never prove it. And also he is in the grip of the need to retaliate. And he is a pacifist. He gets an idea and slips out again into the dark.

They found Bruns the next morning, all beaten up, drowned, his head and shoulders submerged in the watering trough in Du Toit's side yard. The police found Deon still in bed, in his clothes, hung over and incoherent. Marika was also still in bed, also under the weather, and she also was marked up and made a bad exhibit. They say Deon was struck dumb when they took him outside to show him the body.

Here's what I see. Bruns goes to Deon's, goes to the trough and plunges his head underwater and fills his lungs. I believe he could do it. It would be like he was beaten and pushed under. He was capable of this. He would see himself striking at the centre of the web and convicting Du Toit for a thousand unrecorded crimes. It's self-immolation. It's nonviolent.

Deon protested that he was innocent, but he made some serious mistakes. He got panicky. He tried to contend he was with one of the other families that night, but that story collapsed when somebody else got panicky. Also it led to some perjury charges against the Vissers. Then Deon changed his story, saying how he remembered hearing some noises during the night, going out to see what they were, seeing nothing, and going back in and to bed. This could be the truth, but by the time he said it nobody believed him.

The ruin is absolute. It is a real Götterdämmerung. Deon is in jail, charged, and the least he can get is five years. He will have to eat out of a bucket. The chief is disgraced and they are discussing a regency. Bruns was under his protection, formally, and all the volunteer agencies are upset. In order to defend himself the chief is telling everything he can about how helpless he is in fact in Keteng, because the real power is with the seven families. He's pouring out details, so there are going to be charges against the families on other grounds, mostly about bribery and taxes. Also, an election is coming, so the local member of Parliament has a chance to be zealous about white citizens acting like they're outside the law. Business licences are getting suspended. Theunis Pieters is selling out. There's a new police compound going up and more police coming in. They're posting a magistrate.

There is ruin. It's perfect.

Götterdämmerung: the twilight of the gods; the violent end of everything.

JULIE SCHUMACHER

Reunion

'Reunion' is the first story that Julie Schumacher has published, originally
as a prize-winner in a university magazine. She comes from Delaware and
has a master's degree from Cornell.

This too is a family story – a family where the women live long and are
the strength; father has his problems! The women are proud of their long
lives and love to meet every year. Other reunions can come to seem more
important, however.

It wasn't till years after the operation that I realized my mother
would never have died from it. She came from a long line of unscru-
pulously healthy women who had dedicated their entire lives to
surpassing each other in maturity. They no longer counted their age
in years, but in reunions, and nothing under fifty was counted at
all.

My mother lived for the reunions. Every year and a half she would
dress up and lead us, trembling and fearful, to the skirts of our
grandmothers, great-grandmothers and great-aunts. They towered
over us at an impressive height, their legs thickly swathed in flesh-
coloured stockings. My sister and I were left to ourselves during the
ceremonies; we looked wistfully on while the women were photo-
graphed, smiling and blowing out huge numbers of birthday candles, more set against the idea of death every day. Their pictures
still hang on our living room wall, so close together a finger can't fit
between the frames.

It was the first time that any woman in the family had gone into a
hospital. My cousins wouldn't even go there to give birth for fear

people would suspect them of going for something else. Naturally my mother was questioned, cajoled and warned against the dangers of lost reputation, but she went anyway, taking the largest of the reunion photographs in her suitcase. It was a newspaper clipping of her great-grandmother's sisters seated around a silver trophy bearing the slogan of the American Longevity Association. Their names were listed in order of age in the caption.

My mother left on Thursday. The only thing she said before she shut the door was, 'Take care of your father.' She always worried about him.

'What for?' said my sister. She and I were the only ones home with him and didn't know how to take care of a fifty-five-year-old man. We didn't want her to go away; at a distance she would seem more vulnerable. Anything that happened to her would be our fault, anything we did wrong was bound to cause her pain.

My father took it harder than any of us. He hadn't really expected her to go, and just the day before he'd made her angry by pointing out that 'hospitalization' would go down on her work record. He wasn't trying to hurt her; he only wanted to know where the pain was.

'Is it something to do with your . . . being female?' he asked, spotting me in the doorway.

She told him it wasn't, that it was something much less serious than he could imagine, and that certainly didn't deserve to be on a permanent record.

'Why should I have to imagine? Why don't you tell me so I don't have to imagine?'

'I'm much stronger than you might think.' She was already making arrangements to take her Christmas vacation in August.

'What will I do while you're gone? What will the kids do? What will they think?' His voice warbled.

'They know there's nothing wrong with their mother.' She smiled at me and I thought of all the times I'd stepped on the sidewalk cracks and then gone back to erase them, rubbing the soles of my shoes sideways along the pavement. 'And I've already provided for your food.'

When she wouldn't tell him the name of the hospital he accused her of making it all up.

'Why are you bothering with all this?' he asked her.

She was silent so he turned to me.

'Your mother isn't like anyone else,' he said.

When we told him she'd gone he called all the hospitals until he tracked her down at Northern Memorial, but the operator said my mother's number was unlisted.

'What room is she in?' he asked.

'I'm not allowed to give out that information,' said the operator.

'Well how big is your hospital?'

'Thirty-six floors.'

My father was dumbfounded. 'Do you know what she's in for?' he asked.

The operator said she didn't know.

My mother called the next day, but wouldn't give us her room or phone number. She said she was fine. She didn't want any visitors, and told us not to send flowers, the room was full of them from the families of other patients. (The flowers we'd already sent were later returned in a cellophane bag, a note taped to the outside with the message: 'Put these in the dining room – big yellow vase ¾ full of sugar water.') She asked about my father and we told her he was angry about the unlisted number and didn't want to talk. She sighed, told us to watch that he didn't get upset.

My father was furious.

'She didn't even *ask* to talk to me?'

'No, she just asked how you were. She told us to watch out for you.'

He didn't want to know anything more about it. He had the extension wired for the next time she called so that he could hear without being heard, and he would answer all her questions while laughing to himself that she didn't know he was listening.

Once in a while the woman who shared my mother's room would call for her, explaining that my mother was busy – getting signatures on a petition for fresh vegetables on the lunch trays. We did not know what to say to the woman, but felt obligated to talk to her since my mother had asked her to call.

'What are you in for?' we asked her.

'I'm a kidney patient,' she said.

'Kidneys?' said my father, shouting into the dead mouthpiece.

'Your mother's a very nice person. She talks to everyone,' said the woman.

'What does she say?'

'She talks about sports and politics, you know.'

'Well tell her we said hello.'

'Tell her we don't want to talk to any more kidney patients,' said my father.

When my mother called back she wanted to know how my father was doing. 'Does he ask about me very often?' she said.

I looked at my father's back in the hallway. He was sitting on the floor with the extension to his ear, his legs spread straight in front of him. He looked like a bear in a picture I'd seen once.

'All the time,' I said, and I saw him shift the extension to his other ear.

One day I found him staring at the space left on the wall where my mother had taken the picture.

'Something's missing,' he told me.

'She took it with her,' I said.

'There are no men on this wall,' said my father, ignoring me.

I looked. There were no men on the wall. The men in my mother's family weren't important; no one knew anything about them except who they were married to, and as soon as they'd produced a few children they seemed to disappear. On the other hand it was well known that my maternal grandmother had once set fire to her own home rather than see it knocked down, and at the height of the blaze, jumped out a second-storey window to the ground, her eighty-three-year-old legs sturdy as a cat's when she landed. My great-grandmother came to America on a freight ship, disguised as a sailor, and before reaching shore had been promoted to first mate.

'I guess the women live to be older,' I said.

'It looks like a family of clones,' he said. 'Not a man in the group. There's no pictures of your mother either.'

I looked. Everyone in the pictures was at least sixty-five. 'She's probably not old enough,' I said.

He searched the house until he found a picture of my mother, and then he put it on the coffee table. It showed her gardening, leaning over the tomato bushes in the back yard, perspiration stains up and down the back of her shirt. It was a good likeness. She seemed about to stand up, and the way she bent over the tomatoes made her look even stronger than usual. She could have been an advertisement for vegetables. Photographs always had a way of immortalizing her; even when she was standing next to me I'd imagine her in a different pose. I had a collection of them in my head, and she was different in every one.

My great-grandmothers brought us casseroles and desserts, dropping them off on the step after dark so the neighbours wouldn't see them and start asking questions. They must have been communicating with my mother in spite of their disapproval; one dish of manicotti came over with a tiny envelope on its lid, and the note inside said: 'I never use ricotta cheese, it's too expensive. Cottage cheese is just as good and I'm sure they won't know the difference. M.' We passed it once around the table and let the dog lick the dishes. My father got angry because we didn't leave enough on our plates.

'Jesus Christ, what's the dog supposed to live on?' he shouted.

It was obvious the strain was affecting him. He still refused to talk to my mother on the phone, but he started giving us lists of questions to ask her: whether the doctors were men or women and how old they were, how many people shared her room, how many times a day she got to eat . . . Sometimes he would sit with the receiver to his ear for hours after she'd hung up, and whenever I walked by him in the hallway he would block my path with his legs and ask me another question.

The next time my mother called she said we shouldn't expect her to call so often, that she wouldn't be calling for two or three days. She said she'd be having an operation, a small one, but that everything was fine, there was no reason to worry.

My father almost tore the extension from the wall. He started shouting into the receiver saying she'd promised it wasn't serious, saying she had to come home immediately. She could hear his voice from the echoes bouncing into the kitchen, and she shouted back, 'I'm fine, Frederick, they're just going to fix me up a little.' When the echoes subsided she said, 'Tell your father I'll be fine.'

He didn't believe it. He told us all the horror stories he'd ever heard about hospitals.

'During the war there was a man,' he said, 'a Polish general, who was so weak he couldn't eat. By the end of a month he was shrunken beyond recognition. They'd starved him almost to death, and it was up to his wife to get him out of the country. She had to wrap him in blankets and pull him across the border in a toy wagon.'

'You mean she disguised him as a baby and nobody could tell he was really an old man?' we asked.

'He wasn't supposed to look like a baby,' said my father. 'How could a sixty-year-old man look like a baby? You're missing the whole point.'

'Well what does it have to do with Mommy's operation anyway?'

He shook his head as if we were being stupid.

The day of the operation I found him hanging a picture in the empty space on the wall. It was a photograph of an old man wearing a brown coat and a bland expression.

'Who's that?' said my sister.

'My Uncle Jack. He lived to be eighty-seven.'

'That doesn't sound very old,' we said.

'Just by comparison. No one in your mother's family ever dies. People in my family die early.'

'What do they die of?' we asked.

'That's beside the point.' He walked to the opposite wall, took a picture of my mother out of his wallet, and tucked its edges into the corner of a reunion photograph, smoothing it down with his thumb. 'Way beside the point.' It was a newspaper clipping of my mother on the median strip of a highway, a white flag tied to the antenna of her broken-down VW. The picture was taken by a helicopter during the worst traffic jam of the year, and my mother was looking up and waving just when the camera clicked. She was just big enough so that I could recognize her.

'What does all this have to do with Mommy's operation anyway?'

'You don't like the picture?' said my father.

'That's not the point,' I said.

'No, I guess it isn't,' he agreed.

She came home on a Saturday. The front yard was covered with blackbirds fighting over crusts of pizza we'd thrown out the night before, and as my mother walked over the grass she shooed them away, picking up the crusts and bringing them in the house. 'What have you been eating all this time?' she asked, waving the mutilated crusts in front of her. My father took her by the hand and sat her down on the couch. She had a long red scar across the front of her neck.

He was speechless. This had never happened before; it was the first scar in the family, the end of an era.

'Did it hurt?' he asked, finally.

She got up and walked over to the mirror. The scar went straight across the front of her throat, but wasn't obvious unless she tipped her head back. She tilted her head carefully, still looking in the mirror, and ran her fingers over the bluish-red skin, pulling lightly down with one finger and up with another.

'Does it hurt now?' asked my father.

'No.' She turned and saw the picture of Uncle Jack on the wall. 'Who's this?'

'No one,' said my father.

'Why is he hanging on the wall then?'

'He's the one they dressed up as a baby,' my sister told her.

'He was *not* dressed up as a baby,' shouted my father. 'That was *not* the reason for the toy wagon.'

He turned to my mother, who had just discovered her own picture. She took it down and put it between the encyclopaedias.

'Are you sure it doesn't hurt?' he asked again.

We worried about her from then on. She slept a lot. My father rented a mechanical bed for the living room and we took turns raising and lowering her legs. We never pushed the button that moved her neck even when she said it didn't hurt.

When she started talking about the next reunion, and said she wanted to be in the picture, my two great-grandmothers came over to talk her out of it. They saw the mechanical bed and looked politely away.

'You're not even grey yet,' they said. They saw the picture of Uncle Jack and squinted.

'I want to be in the picture,' said my mother.

'Aunt Gladys thought you were dead and buried.'

'I want to be in the picture,' she repeated.

They sighed. 'Do you have something with a high neck?'

My mother nodded.

Two months later it was on the living room wall. Uncle Jack had been taken down, and in his place stood my mother, dressed in a blue turtleneck. The scar was completely hidden. Since she was off to one side it was hard to tell whether she was meant to be in the picture or if she'd just walked in by accident. But she looked beautiful, and my sister and I imagined her in blue for a long time.

Aunt Gladys had come up after the candles were blown out. 'I thought you were dead and buried,' she said, clutching my mother's arm. 'What a relief.'

Eventually the scar lost its colour and settled into a fold in my mother's skin. She said the doctors told her not to drive; the bones in the back of her neck will always be weak.

It wasn't till years afterward that I realized my mother would never have died from it. At night she still stands by my bed in the dark, telling me not to worry. Whenever she leaves the house, or pulls the car out of the garage, I tell myself, my mother is stronger than anyone else's.

I see her driving down the highway, she waves to me and my heart swells. I see her crashing into the car just in front, her whole neck giving away, her head faltering, my mother, the car crossing over the median and bursting into . . . No. It was only a small accident, she's all right, it didn't hurt for a minute. There's my mother standing on the median, safely out of the wreck, thumbing a ride. I know she won't slip, the trucks going by won't even come near her, and soon, someone will roll down their window and offer to take her home. She waves once more and the helicopter pulls back, snaps another picture, another, farther and farther away until she's just a normal woman on a highway, no one's mother, no scar on her neck at all. Cars speed past in both directions, here she is by my bed, her hands cool on my back in the dark. We can sleep peacefully, knowing my mother is immortal. There she is on the highway, there in the yard, leaning over tomato bushes in the garden, and I can bring her back whenever I need her.

SAM SHEPARD

Motel Chronicles (an excerpt)

Sam Shepard is a dramatist and a scriptwriter for films. The collection of pieces from which this little story is taken is, in part, observations, poems, thoughts that are background to a film of his.

No wonder the boy's father was angry, you may think. It had been a dangerous escapade, not like taking 'a short vacation'! The tunnel *did* have an end.

The first time I ran away from school I was ten. Two older guys talked me into it. They were brothers and they'd both been in and out of Juvenile Hall five times. They told me it would just be like taking a short vacation. So I went. We stole three bikes out of a back yard and took off for the Arroyo Seco. The bike I stole was too big for me so I could never sit up on the seat all the way. I pedalled standing.

We hid the bikes in a stand of Eucalyptus trees at the edge of the Arroyo and went down to the creek. We caught Crawdads with marshmallow bait then tore the shells off them and used their meat to catch more Crawdads. When lunch time came I had to share my lunch with the brothers because they'd forgotten to bring theirs. I spread the contents of the paper bag out on a big flat rock. A carrot wrapped in wax paper with a rubber band around it. A meatloaf sandwich. A melted bag of M and Ms. They ate the M and Ms first. Tore the package open and licked the chocolate off the paper. They offered me a lick but I declined. I didn't eat any of the meatloaf

Juvenile Hall: they were in care.
Crawdads: crayfish.
M and Ms: a brand of sugar-coated chocolate drops.

sandwich either. I always hated meatloaf. Especially cold and between bread.

The rest of the afternoon we climbed around in the hills looking for snakes until one of them got the idea of lowering our bikes down into the aqueduct and riding along the dry bed until we reached Los Angeles. I said 'yes' to everything even though I suspected LA was at least a hundred miles away. The only other time I'd ever been to Los Angeles was when my Aunt took me to the Farmer's Market in her '45 Dodge to look at the Myna birds. I must have been six then.

I climbed the chain-link barrier fence while the two brothers took the tension out of the barb-wire strands at the top. Enough so I could straddle the fence, get one foot on the concrete wall of the aqueduct and drop some ten or twelve feet to the bottom. Then they lowered the bikes down to me, suspended on their belts. We rode for miles down this giant corridor of cement, the wheels of our bikes bumping over the brown lines of caulking used to seal the seams. Except for those seams it was the smoothest, flattest surface I'd ever ridden a bike on.

We rode past red shotgun shells faded by the sun, dead opossums, beer cans, Walnut shells, Carob pods, a Raccoon with two babies, pages out of porno magazines, hunks of rope, inner tubes, hub caps, bottle caps, dried-up Sage plants, boards with nails, stumps, roots, smashed glass, yellow golf balls with red stripes, a lug wrench, women's underwear, tennis shoes, dried-up socks, a dead dog, mice, Dragon Flies screwing in mid-air, shrivelled-up frogs with their eyes popped out. We rode for miles until we came to a part that was all enclosed like a big long tunnel and we couldn't see light at the other end. We stopped our bikes and stared through the mouth of that tunnel and I could tell they were just as scared as I was even though they were older. It was already starting to get dark and the prospect of getting stuck in there at night, not knowing how long the thing was or what town we'd come out in or how in the hell we were going to climb back out once we came to the end of it, had us all wishing we were back home. None of us said we wished that but I could feel it passing between us.

I don't remember how the decision was made but we pushed off straight ahead into it. The floor was concave and slick with moss, causing the wheels to slip sideways. Sometimes our feet came down ankle-deep in sludge and black mud and we ended up having to walk the bikes through most of it. We kept making sounds to each other just to keep track of where we were as the light disappeared behind us. We started out trying to scare each other with weird noises but gave it up because the echoes were truly terrifying. I kept having visions of Los Angeles appearing suddenly at the other end of the tunnel. It would just pop up at us, all blinking with lights and movement and life. Sometimes it would appear like I'd seen it in postcards. (Palm Trees set against a background of snowy mountains with orange groves sprawling beneath them. The Train Station with a burro standing in front of it, harnessed to a cart.) But it didn't come. For hours it didn't come. And my feet were wet. And I forgot what the two brothers even looked like anymore. I kept having terrible thoughts about home. About what would happen when I finally got back. In the blackness I pictured our house. The red awning. The garage door. The strip of lawn down the centre of the driveway. The Pyracantha berries. The Robins that ate them. Close-ups of the Robin's beak guzzling red berries. So close I could see little dribbles of dirt from wet lawns where he'd been pulling out worms. I couldn't stop these pictures. (Me walking to school. The chubby old Crossing Guard at the corner with his round wooden sign that read STOP in red letters. The dirt playground. Porcelain water fountains with silver knobs dribbling. The face of the kid I hit in the stomach for no reason. Little traces of mayonnaise around his lips.) I had the feeling these pictures would drown me. I wondered what the two brothers were thinking but I never asked them.

It was night when we reached the end and it wasn't Los Angeles either. Huge Sycamore trees with hazy orange street lights loomed over our heads. We could hear the sound of a freeway. Periodic whooshing of trucks. We hauled ourselves out by climbing on each other's shoulders and hooking the belts to the top of the fence. The oldest brother said he recognized the town we were in. He said it was Sierra Madre and he had an Uncle who lived pretty close by. We pedalled to his Uncle's house and we weren't talking to each other at that point. There was nothing to say.

His Uncle lived in a small three-room house with several men sitting around the front room drinking beer and watching the Lone Ranger on TV. Nobody seemed surprised to see us. They acted like

Lone Ranger: the cowboy hero of a television series of westerns, made for children in the early sixties.

this had happened a lot before. A woman was making a big pot of spaghetti in the kitchen and she gave us each a paper plate and told us to wait for the meat sauce to heat up. We sat on the floor at the feet of the men in the front room and watched the Lone Ranger and ate spaghetti. That was the first time I'd ever seen TV because we didn't have one at home. (My Dad said we didn't need one.) I liked the Lone Ranger a lot. Especially the music when he galloped on Silver and reared up waving his hat at a woman holding a baby.

We were finally caught later that night by a squad car on a bridge in South Pasadena. The cops acted like we were adults. They had that kind of serious tone: 'Where did you get these bikes? What are your names? Where do you live? Do you know what time it is?' Stuff like that. They radioed our parents and confiscated the bikes. My mother showed up and drove me back, explaining how my Dad was so pissed off that he wouldn't come because he was afraid he'd kill me. She kept saying, 'Now you've got a Police Record. You'll have that the rest of your life.'

I got whipped three times with the buckle-end of my Dad's belt. Three times. That was it. Then he left the house. He never said a word.

I lay in bed listening to my mother ironing in the kitchen. I pictured her ironing. The hiss of steam. The sprinkle bottle she used to wet my Dad's shirts. I pictured her face staring down at the shirt as her arm moved back and forth in a steady tempo.

KURT VONNEGUT Jr

Tom Edison's Shaggy Dog

Kurt Vonnegut is not altogether a science-fiction writer, though he does create other worlds that can cast a harsh light on ours. He is something of a humorist. Here, among other things, we find out how not to be boring about a bore. Perhaps, too, a way to deflect a bore. You, of course, will have to see what happens with the intelligence analyser, and if you do not get the point about the shaggy dog, then ask around . . . why spoil it for you now?

Two old men sat on a park bench one morning in the sunshine of Tampa, Florida – one trying doggedly to read a book he was plainly enjoying while the other, Harold K. Bullard, told him the story of his life in the full, round, head tones of a public address system. At their feet lay Bullard's Labrador retriever, who further tormented the aged listener by probing his ankles with a large, wet nose.

Bullard, who had been, before he retired, successful in many fields, enjoyed reviewing his important past. But he faced the problem that complicates the lives of cannibals – namely: that a single victim cannot be used over and over. Anyone who had passed the time of day with him and his dog refused to share a bench with them again.

So Bullard and his dog set out through the park each day in quest of new faces. They had had good luck this morning, for they had found this stranger right away, clearly a new arrival in Florida, still buttoned up tight in heavy serge, stiff collar and necktie, and with nothing better to do than read.

'Yes,' said Bullard, rounding out the first hour of his lecture, 'made and lost fortunes in my time.'

'So you said,' said the stranger, whose name Bullard had neglected to ask. 'Easy, boy. No, no, no, boy,' he said to the dog, who was growing more aggressive toward his ankles.

'Oh? Already told you that, did I?' said Bullard.

'Twice.'

'Two in real estate, one in scrap iron, and one in oil and one in trucking.'

'So you said.'

'I did? Yes, I guess I did. Two in real estate, one in scrap iron, one in oil, and one in trucking. Wouldn't take back a day of it.'

'No, I suppose not,' said the stranger. 'Pardon me, but do you suppose you could move your dog somewhere else? He keeps –'

'Him?' said Bullard, heartily. 'Friendliest dog in the world. Don't need to be afraid of him.'

'I'm not afraid of him. It's just that he drives me crazy, sniffing at my ankles.'

'Plastic,' said Bullard, chuckling.

'What?'

'Plastic. Must be something plastic on your garters. By golly, I'll bet it's those little buttons. Sure as we're sitting here, those buttons must be plastic. That dog is nuts about plastic. Don't know why that is, but he'll sniff it out and find it if there's a speck around. Must be a deficiency in his diet, though, by gosh, he eats better than I do. Once he chewed up a whole plastic humidor. Can you beat it? *That's* the business I'd go into now, by glory, if the pill rollers hadn't told me to let up, to give the old ticker a rest.'

'You could tie the dog to that tree over there,' said the stranger.

'I get so darn' sore at all the youngsters these days!' said Bullard. 'All of 'em mooning around about no frontiers any more. There never have been so many frontiers as there are today. You know what Horace Greeley would say today?'

'His nose is wet,' said the stranger, and he pulled his ankles away, but the dog humped forward in patient pursuit. 'Stop it, boy!'

'His wet nose shows he's healthy,' said Bullard. ' "Go plastic, young man!" That's what Greeley'd say. "Go atom, young man!" '

The dog had definitely located the plastic buttons on the stranger's garters and was cocking his head one way and another, thinking out ways of bringing his teeth to bear on those delicacies.

'Scat!' said the stranger.

' "Go electronic, young man!" ' said Bullard. 'Don't talk to me about no opportunity any more. Opportunity's knocking down every door in the country, trying to get in. When I was young, a man had to go out and find opportunity and drag it home by the ears. Nowadays –'

'Sorry,' said the stranger, evenly. He slammed his book shut, stood and jerked his ankle away from the dog. 'I've got to be on my way. So good day, sir.'

He stalked across the park, found another bench, sat down with a sigh and began to read. His respiration had just returned to normal, when he felt the wet sponge of the dog's nose on his ankles again.

'Oh – it's you!' said Bullard, sitting down beside him. 'He was tracking you. He was on the scent of something, and I just let him have his head. What'd I tell you about plastic?' He looked about contentedly. 'Don't blame you for moving on. It was stuffy back there. No shade to speak of and not a sign of a breeze.'

'Would the dog go away if I bought him a humidor?' said the stranger.

'Pretty good joke, pretty good joke,' said Bullard, amiably. Suddenly he clapped the stranger on his knee. 'Sa-ay, you aren't in plastics, are you? Here I've been blowing off about plastics, and for all I know that's your line.'

'My line?' said the stranger crisply, laying down his book. 'Sorry – I've never had a line. I've been a drifter since the age of nine, since Edison set up his laboratory next to my home, and showed me the intelligence analyser.'

'Edison?' said Bullard. 'Thomas Edison, the inventor?'

'If you want to call him that, go ahead,' said the stranger.

'If I *want* to call him that?' – Bullard guffawed – 'I guess I just will! Father of the light bulb and I don't know what all.'

'If you want to think he invented the light bulb, go ahead. No harm in it.' The stranger resumed his reading.

'Say, what is this?' said Bullard, suspiciously. 'You pulling my leg? What's this about an intelligence analyser? I never heard of that.'

'Of course you haven't,' said the stranger. 'Mr Edison and I promised to keep it a secret. I've never told anyone. Mr Edison broke his promise and told Henry Ford, but Ford made him promise not to tell anybody else – for the good of humanity.'

Bullard was entranced. 'Uh, this intelligence analyser,' he said, 'it analysed intelligence, did it?'

'It was an electric butter churn,' said the stranger.

'Seriously now,' Bullard coaxed.

'Maybe it *would* be better to talk it over with someone,' said the stranger. 'It's a terrible thing to keep bottled up inside me, year in and year out. But how can I be sure that it won't go any further?'

'My word as a gentleman,' Bullard assured him.

'I don't suppose I could find a stronger guarantee than that, could I?' said the stranger, judiciously.

'There is no stronger guarantee,' said Bullard, proudly. 'Cross my heart and hope to die!'

'Very well.' The stranger leaned back and closed his eyes, seeming to travel backwards through time. He was silent for a full minute, during which Bullard watched with respect.

'It was back in the fall of eighteen seventy-nine,' said the stranger at last, softly. 'Back in the village of Menlo Park, New Jersey. I was a boy of nine. A young man we all thought was a wizard had set up a laboratory next door to my home, and there were flashes and crashes inside, and all sorts of scary goings-on. The neighbourhood children were warned to keep away, not to make any noise that would bother the wizard.

'I didn't get to know Edison right off, but his dog Sparky and I got to be steady pals. A dog a whole lot like yours, Sparky was, and we used to wrestle all over the neighbourhood. Yes, sir, your dog is the image of Sparky.'

'Is that so?' said Bullard, flattered.

'Gospel,' replied the stranger. 'Well, one day Sparky and I were wrestling around, and we wrestled right up to the door of Edison's laboratory. The next thing I knew, Sparky had pushed me in through the door, and bam! I was sitting on the laboratory floor, looking up at Mr Edison himself.'

'Bet he was sore,' said Bullard, delighted.

'You can bet I was scared,' said the stranger. 'I thought I was face to face with Satan himself. Edison had wires hooked to his ears and running down to a little black box in his lap! I started to scoot, but he caught me by the collar and made me sit down.

' "Boy," said Edison, "it's always darkest before the dawn. I want you to remember that."

' "Yes, sir," I said.

' "For over a year, my boy," Edison said to me, "I've been trying to find a filament that will last in an incandescent lamp. Hair, string, splinters – nothing works. So while I was trying to think of something else to try, I started tinkering about with another idea of mine, just letting off steam. I put this together," he said, showing me the little black box. "I thought maybe intelligence was just a certain kind of electricity, so I made this intelligence analyser here. It works! You're the first one to know about it, my boy. But I don't know why you shouldn't be. It will be your generation that will grow up in the glorious new era when people will be as easily graded as oranges." '

'I don't believe it!' said Bullard.

'May I be struck by lightning this very instant!' said the stranger. 'And it did work, too. Edison had tried out the analyser on the men in his shop, without telling them what he was up to. The smarter a man was, by gosh, the farther the needle on the indicator in the little black box swung to the right. I let him try it on me, and the needle just lay where it was and trembled. But dumb as I was, then is when I made my one and only contribution to the world. As I say, I haven't lifted a finger since.'

'Whadja do?' said Bullard, eagerly.

'I said, "Mr Edison, sir, let's try it on the dog." And I wish you could have seen the show that dog put on when I said it! Old Sparky barked and howled and scratched to get out. When he saw we meant business, that he wasn't going to get out, he made a beeline right for the intelligence analyser and knocked it out of Edison's hands. But we cornered him, and Edison held him down while I touched the wires to his ears. And would you believe it, that needle sailed clear across the dial, way past a little red pencil mark on the dial face!'

'The dog busted it,' said Bullard.

' "Mr Edison, sir," I said, "what's that red mark mean?"

' "My boy," said Edison, "it means that the instrument is broken, because that red mark is me." '

'I'll say it was broken,' said Bullard.

The stranger said gravely, 'But it wasn't broken. No, sir. Edison checked the whole thing, and it was in apple-pie order. When Edison told me that, it was then that Sparky, crazy to get out, gave himself away.'

'How?' said Bullard, suspiciously.

'We really had him locked in, see? There were three locks on the door – a hook and eye, a bolt, and a regular knob and latch. That dog stood up, unhooked the hook, pushed the bolt back and had the knob in his teeth when Edison stopped him.'

'No!' said Bullard.

'Yes!' said the stranger, his eyes shining. 'And then is when Edison showed me what a great scientist he was. He was willing to face the truth, no matter how unpleasant it might be.

' "So!" said Edison to Sparky. "Man's best friend, huh? Dumb animal, huh?"

'That Sparky was a caution. He pretended not to hear. He scratched himself and bit fleas and went around growling at rat-holes – anything to get out of looking Edison in the eye.

' "Pretty soft, isn't it, Sparky?" said Edison. "Let somebody else worry about getting food, building shelters and keeping warm, while you sleep in front of a fire or go chasing after the girls or raise hell with the boys. No mortgages, no politics, no war, no work, no worry. Just wag the old tail or lick a hand, and you're all taken care of."

' "Mr Edison," I said, "do you mean to tell me that dogs are smarter than people?"

' "Smarter?" said Edison. "I'll tell the world! And what have I been doing for the past year? Slaving to work out a light bulb so dogs can play at night!"

' "Look, Mr Edison," said Sparky, "Why not –" '

'Hold on!' roared Bullard.

'Silence!' shouted the stranger, triumphantly. ' "Look, Mr Edison," said Sparky, "why not keep quiet about this? It's been working out to everybody's satisfaction for hundreds of thousands of years. Let sleeping dogs lie. You forget all about it, destroy the intelligence analyser, and I'll tell you what to use for a lamp filament." '

'Hogwash!' said Bullard, his face purple.

The stranger stood. 'You have my solemn word as a gentleman. That dog rewarded *me* for my silence with a stockmarket tip that made me independently wealthy for the rest of my days. And the last words that Sparky ever spoke were to Thomas Edison. "Try a piece of carbonized cotton thread," he said. Later, he was torn to bits by a pack of dogs that had gathered outside the door, listening.'

The stranger removed his garters and handed them to Bullard's dog. 'A small token of esteem, sir, for an ancestor of yours who talked himself to death. Good day.' He tucked his book under his arm and walked away.

Acknowledgements

The publishers make grateful acknowledgement to the following for permission to reprint:

Isaac Asimov, 'Star Light', reprinted by permission of the author, © Hoffman Electronics Corporation, 1962.

Gina Berriault, 'The Stone Boy', reprinted from *The Mistress and Other Stories* (E. P. Dutton Inc.) by permission of Laurence Pollinger Ltd.

Fredric Brown, 'The Solipsist', reprinted from *Angels and Spaceships* (E. P. Dutton Inc.) by permission of Roberta Pryor Inc., © Fredric Brown, 1954.

Ernest Haycox, 'A Day in Town', reprinted by permission of the author and the author's agents, Scott Meredith Literary Agency, Inc., 845 Third Avenue, New York, New York, 10022.

Shirley Jackson, 'The Pajama Party', from *Come Along With Me*, © Shirley Jackson, 1963. Reprinted by permission of Viking Penguin Inc.

W. P. Kinsella, 'The Thrill of the Grass', from *The Thrill of the Grass*, copyright © W. P. Kinsella, 1984. Reprinted by permission of Viking Penguin Inc. and Penguin Books Canada Ltd.

Ursula Le Guin, 'The Professor's Houses', copyright © Ursula K. Le Guin, 1982. First published in *The New Yorker*. Reprinted by permission of the author and her agent.

Bobbie Ann Mason, 'Graveyard Day', from *Shiloh and Other Stories*, reprinted by permission of Chatto & Windus Ltd and Alfred A. Knopf, Inc.

Wright Morris, 'Victrola', first published in *The New Yorker*. Reprinted by permission of Russell and Volkening, Inc., as agents for the author. Copyright © Wright Morris, 1982.

Joyce Carol Oates, 'Small Avalanches', from *The Goddess and Other Women* (Victor Gollancz), © Joyce Carol Oates, 1975. Reprinted by permission of Murray Pollinger and Blanche C. Gregory Inc.